IT HAPPENED TO ME

Series Editor: Arlene Hirschfelder

Books in the It Happened to Me series are designed for inquisitive teens digging for answers about certain illnesses, social issues, or lifestyle interests. Whether you are deep into your teen years or just entering them, these books are gold mines of up-to-date information, riveting teen views, and great visuals to help you figure out stuff. Besides special boxes highlighting singular facts, each book is enhanced with the latest reading list, websites, and an index. Perfect for browsing, there's loads of expert information by acclaimed writers to help parents, guardians, and librarians understand teen illness, tough situations, and lifestyle choices.

1. *Learning Disabilities: The Ultimate Teen Guide*, by Penny Hutchins Paquette and Cheryl Gerson Tuttle, 2003.
2. *Epilepsy: The Ultimate Teen Guide*, by Kathlyn Gay and Sean McGarrahan, 2002.
3. *Stress Relief: The Ultimate Teen Guide*, by Mark Powell, 2002.
4. *Making Sexual Decisions: The Ultimate Teen Guide*, by L. Kris Gowen, Ph.D., 2003.
5. *Asthma: The Ultimate Teen Guide*, by Penny Hutchins Paquette, 2003.
6. *Cultural Diversity: Conflicts and Challenges: The Ultimate Teen Guide*, by Kathlyn Gay, 2003.
7. *Diabetes: The Ultimate Teen Guide*, by Katherine J. Moran, 2004.
8. *When Will I Stop Hurting? Teens, Loss, and Grief: The Ultimate Teen Guide*, by Edward Myers, 2004.
9. *Volunteering: The Ultimate Teen Guide*, by Kathlyn Gay, 2004.
10. *Organ Transplants: A Survival Guide for the Entire Family: The Ultimate Teen Guide*, by Tina P. Schwartz, 2005.
11. *Medications: The Ultimate Teen Guide*, by Cheryl Gerson Tuttle, 2005.

Money

Getting It, Using It, and Avoiding the Traps: The Ultimate Teen Guide

ROBIN F. BRANCATO

It Happened to Me, No. 18

The Scarecrow Press, Inc.
Lanham, Maryland • Toronto • Plymouth, UK
2007

SCARECROW PRESS, INC.

Published in the United States of America
by Scarecrow Press, Inc.
A wholly owned subsidary of
The Rowman & Littlefield Publishing Group, Inc.
4501 Forbes Boulevard, Suite 200, Lanham, Maryland 20706
www.scarecrowpress.com

Estover Road
Plymouth PL6 7PY
United Kingdom

British Library Cataloguing in Publication Information Available

Library of Congress Cataloging-in-Publication Data

Brancato, Robin F.
    Money : getting it, using it, and avoiding the traps : the ultimate teen guide / Robin F. Brancato.
        p. cm. — (It happened to me ; no. 18)
    Includes bibliographical references and index.
    ISBN-13: 978-0-8108-5632-5 (hardcover : alk. paper)
    ISBN-10: 0-8108-5632-8 (hardcover : alk. paper)
    1. Teenagers—Finance, Personal. 2. Finance, Personal. I. Title.
HG179.B7224 2007
332.02400835—dc22

2006036875

⊗™ The paper used in this publication meets the minimum requirements of
American National Standard for Information Sciences—Permanence of Paper
for Printed Library Materials, ANSI/NISO Z39.48-1992.
Manufactured in the United States of America.

For Clayton, Jason, Francesca, Olivia, and Luca

ODE TO MONEY

George Washington, Abraham Lincoln, Andrew Jackson
The fresh crispness of the bill you receive from the bank
The wrinkled discolored almost ripped ones
You receive as change
Then the emptiness
Where are you, money?
Where are you when there are no bills in my wallet?
When I have no money for lunch
and I hear my stomach growling?
Why do I see you in someone's else's pocket?
Why is someone else holding you in their hands?
Why not me?
When will you come back?
When will we become friends again?
Why, money? Why?
Come back into my wallet
For I need that touch, that smell
I need to feel the crispness
I need you

—Mabel Addai, age 17

HOW MUCH DO YOU KNOW ABOUT BUCKS?*

1. **In the 1500s and 1600s, American colonists used for exchange**

    A. money from the countries they came from.

    B. wampum (shells on a string).

    C. Spanish pieces of eight (silver dollars).

    D. A, B, and C.

2. **The first paper money printed in America was called**

    A. pounds.

    B. continentals.

    C. buffaloes.

    D. denominations.

3. **Congress passed a law establishing a money system using the dollar in the year**

    A. 1692.

    B. 1792.

    C. 1892.

    D. 1992.

4. **The famous face that appears on a U.S. $100 bill is**

    A. George Washington.

    B. Abe Lincoln.

    C. Andrew Jackson.

    D. Ben Franklin.

5. **When paper money gets too old and worn to use, it is**

    A. kept in an underground vault.

    B. shredded.

    C. burned.

    D. recycled.

See answers in appendix.

* Source: Neale S. Godfrey, *Ultimate Kids' Money Book* (New York: Simon & Schuster, 1998).

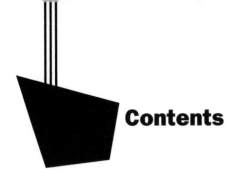

Contents

Contents

Acknowledgments

I would like to thank the students, teachers, and administrators of Teaneck High School, Teaneck, New Jersey, for their willingness to offer me opinions on money and to allow me to observe them in classes. I particularly appreciate the help of students and teachers in business education and English classes. Thanks also to students and teachers of Dwight-Englewood School, Englewood, New Jersey, and of Solomon Schechter High School, New York, and to the individual teenagers I communicated with around the country.

In addition to the *Wall Street Journal Classroom Edition*, source material especially useful to me includes Susan Shelly's *The Complete Idiot's Guide to Money for Teens*, Jayne A. Pearl's *Kids and Money*, and David and Tom Gardner's *The Motley Fool Investment Guide*.

I have been lucky enough, as I worked on this project, to enjoy the research and the writing itself and to profit from the suggestions and support of family members and of several close friends who were interested in this book.

Introduction

ROOT OF ALL EVIL OR POT OF GOLD?

Money talks. And it makes the world go round, right? Or is it the root of all evil? Regardless of how we judge it, almost everybody agrees that we can't function very well without some form of money in a society. And as a young adult you're probably learning fast about the joys and sorrows money can bring. You may be thinking . . . a 9-to-5 job? Stocks and bonds? Interest and taxes? I'll deal with that later. But, chances are, money is already haunting you in some way—stirring up minor waves between you and your family, or your boss, or looming ahead like a major typhoon.

Whether you think about money a little or a lot, the point of this book is to let you know that you aren't alone. You'll find out what others your age have to say about their money experiences so far, and you'll be encouraged to put the right emphasis on money in your life, so that it turns out to be a mostly positive thing. Along the way we'll be looking at how you, now, as a young adult, may get money, use it, and avoid losing it. And because there's such a wealth of information out there about jobs, budgeting, saving, and investing, the special aims of *Money: The Ultimate Teen Guide* will be to trim down these topics to manageable size, to steer you to additional sources if you need them, and to take a look at the ways in which money affects feelings and relationships.

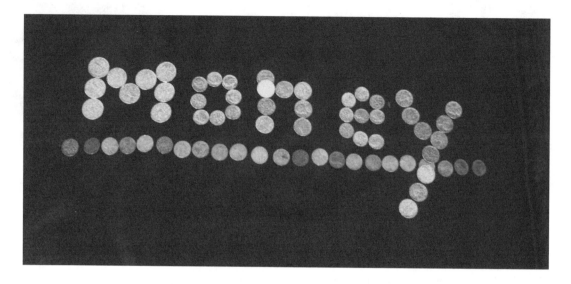

IN THIS BOOK YOU'LL FIND . . .

◎ *The big picture.* What is money? How have money systems changed over the centuries? How did we get from trading shells and beads to swiping credit cards?

◎ *Practical stuff.* What is your present income from allowance, jobs, and windfalls, and how can you increase it and manage it? What's useful to know about checking and savings accounts, investing, and borrowing? What are the traps to avoid as a consumer and as the holder of a credit card?

◎ *Anecdotes and quotes.* What experiences, good and bad, are kids like you having with money? Some might serve as models, others as warnings.

◎ *Questions to ask yourself.* These are guidelines to help you see where you fall on a spectrum so that you can self-correct, if necessary.

The main question to ask yourself as you read is, What should I know concerning money at this point in my life? The emphasis is on school-related situations, part-time jobs, saving and investing, consumer know-how, and money problems that come up in families and among friends. Throughout the book you'll be encouraged to think about the years ahead, and the last chapter will focus specifically on your financial future.

Along the way you'll be referred to additional sources, many of which are on the Internet. For those of you who don't have access to a computer or aren't experienced in going online, there are plenty of recommended books and articles, but for the most up-to-date information you'll want to check out the Net.

The point of *Money: The Ultimate Teen Guide* is to help you use money well. A few kids reading this book may have more money than they need. The majority, probably, will feel they don't have as much as they'd like. Some who have serious money problems may read references to saving, investing, and buying and think, "Are you kidding?" In this country, however, we like to think that everyone has a chance. So the position of this book is that even if the playing field isn't level, with good information, hard work, determination, and a little luck you still have a shot at getting where you want to be.

Lack of money can be annoying, painful, or even tragic, but the other side of the coin is that accumulating and using money sensibly and honestly can be challenging, liberating, and enjoyable. Here's the most important message suggested in this book: Don't let money be your master. Use your knowledge so that you have mastery over it. And whether you have a lot or a little, try to make your money dealings mostly fun.

1 What Is This Thing Called Money?

"If you think about it," Eve Drobot says in *Money, Money, Money*, "money is really an idea, not a thing. Anything can be

A stack of coins. A walletful of bills. A plastic card. A convenience. A necessity. A source of joy and pain. All of the above and more.

used as money as long as everyone agrees it is money. . . . In the very early days, people didn't have money because no one had thought of it yet. They would exchange things for other things. One person would swap a cow, say, for a bag of potatoes and a big pot to cook them in."[1]

WHY MONEY IS CONVENIENT

It's nice to think we could get along without money, but the idea, which has been around for at least 4,000 or 5,000 years, refuses to go away. Then and now, people have generally needed more things than they could produce themselves, so in order to survive they began to swap goods and services. And when bartering got too complicated—is one tent worth *two* camels or *three* camels?—people agreed to use various things as mediums of exchange. In ancient Ethiopia, for instance, they used blocks of salt as money, and in the South Pacific Islands they used whales' teeth and bird feathers. On Yap Island, money stones that weigh more than 500 pounds are still used

GOLD LASTS

▶ Gold has been good for trading because it looks nice, is easy to shape, and is rare.
▶ The first coins (more than 2,000 years ago) were little bean-shaped Lydian coins made of gold mixed with silver.
▶ Hunger for gold caused the Spanish to slaughter 50,000 Aztecs and steal 13 tons of gold jewelry, statues, and religious artifacts from the Incas.
▶ The biggest gold rush in the world took place in California in 1849.
▶ The world's largest stash of gold these days is 7,000 tons, worth about $100 billion, stored in the subbasement of the Federal Reserve Bank in New York City.

for ceremonial transactions—available and durable, but not very convenient.

No one knows which people used coins first—maybe the Sumerians, in the land that is now Iraq and Syria. Gold, of course, has lasted through the centuries as a medium of exchange. Paper money was used in China as long as 2,000 years ago, but in Western countries people felt safer with coins

Gold bricks, or bullion, seen in a Seattle, Washington, Gold Rush museum.

until the 1600s.[2] It took another few centuries for human beings to come up with credit cards. What will be next?

Money is useful. If we had no needs or wants we might never have invented it. But human beings, as you know, have a lot of needs and wants. Are we too acquisitive—that is, do we put too much emphasis on getting? Or, when we acquire things, are we just assembling our own personal survival kits?

Human beings, by the way, aren't the only self-interested animals, and we're not the only animals with an urge to master money matters. Keith Chen, a behavioral economist at Yale University, has taught seven capuchin moneys in a laboratory to use "money."[3] They've learned that certain one-inch silver discs can be exchanged for grapes and Jell-O cubes. This skill isn't just a trick, Chen says, but shows an actual understanding of economics. The monkeys respond to incentives, are wary of risky gambles, fail to save, steal from each other, and use money to "buy" food. Chen's experiment suggests that maybe the urge to get and spend is built into the DNA of all living creatures.

Just as ancient cultures chose different forms of money, modern countries each have their own monetary systems. The term *dollar*, from the German word *thaler*, is used today in 23 countries (from Australia to Zimbabwe), but having a common name doesn't mean that the dollar is worth the same amount everywhere.

WHO DECIDES WHAT MONEY IS WORTH?

Money is worth what people decide it's worth. Things people need and want have high value, and things they don't want so badly are worth less. This is known as the law of supply and demand. Throughout the world, over time, a certain coin or bill may buy more or less than it used to. If a dollar buys less this year than in the past—that's inflation. Inflation is caused by increases in demand and/or costs of production. And if incomes don't keep pace with rising prices, people often suffer badly from inflation. In modern times countries often try to stop inflation by controlling prices, wages, and rules of borrowing.

"Money is only money when it's in motion."

MONEY IN MOTION

If it's just sitting there, it isn't money. The German sociologist
Georg Simmel said that money is only money when it's in
motion. That is, it has to be in use. A stash of dollar bills hidden
under a mattress might as well be old pieces of paper. Also, for
money systems to work, we all have to agree on the value of the
dollar, or the euro (European Community), or the yen (Japan),
or the ruble (Russia), or the shilling (Kenya), or the austral
(Argentina). "Money is built on motion and trust."[4]

HOW MUCH MONEY IS ENOUGH?

Almost everybody accepts the idea that we need money and
that life is better for people who have enough to pay for basic
necessities. Arguments begin, however, when we raise questions
such as, How much money is enough? Is there such a thing as
some people having too much? Should governments regulate
money and business so that everyone's income is more or less
equal? Arguments about these matters go on among historians,

economists, politicians, philosophers, and ordinary people, and disagreements over money have led to out-and-out wars. In short, some believe we all profit if everybody has about the same amount of money. Others are convinced that when we're encouraged to compete—that is, to earn and accumulate as much as possible—we become our best selves.

CAN MONEY BUY HAPPINESS?

Economists find that the more a nation produces, the happier its population. Wealthy nations, however, are usually democracies with fair legal systems, good health care, and honest government. So, are the citizens of those countries happy because they have more money or because they're benefiting from good social services?[5]

Individuals usually become happier if they go from unemployment and homelessness to a job and a home, but other than that, getting richer doesn't buy much extra happiness. An analysis of 150 studies on wealth and happiness shows that even though economic output has increased over past decades, people aren't any more satisfied with their lives. In fact, they even report an increase in depression and mistrust. As you might suspect, most people say that real happiness comes from social relationships, enjoyable work, fulfillment, a sense of meaning in life, and membership in groups.[6]

Young people agree with adults about money and happiness. "Nearly half of American teens believe the American Dream is to be happy. That's more than the number who think it involves owning a house or their own business." In a 2005 poll, almost half of teens surveyed defined the American Dream as "simply being happy, whatever you do." In spite of the popularity of TV shows focused on the rich and famous, only one in five teens equated the American Dream with wealth and fame.[7]

NOT EVERYONE ACHIEVES THE DREAM

Unfortunately, in a country famous for great opportunity and physical comforts, 12.7 percent of citizens, in 2004, lived in poverty. (The official definition of poverty is based on income, size of family, and other criteria.) That percentage translates into 37 million individuals—including many children—or 7.9 million families living in poverty. Further bad news is that those numbers represent an increase in poverty over the previous year. As you might suspect, the poverty rate for certain minorities is higher than for whites, even though Americans claim to value equality of opportunity.[8] What do you think about poverty in a land of wealth and opportunity—is it just the way things are, or is it an embarrassment and a disgrace?

In short, money is an idea, a reality, and a necessity. And just like capuchin monkeys, we seem to be programmed to use it to try to get what we want. Putting money ahead of relationships and enjoyment of work usually results in loneliness and discontent. The trick is to learn how to make money a positive element in your life.

NOTES

1. Eve Drobot, *Money, Money, Money: Where It Comes From, How to Save It, Spend It, and Make It* (Toronto: Maple Leaf Press, 2004), 6.

2. Neale S. Godfrey, *Ultimate Kids' Money Book* (New York: Simon & Schuster, 1998), 15.

3. Stephen J. Dubner and Steven D. Levitt, "Monkey Business," in "Freakonomics," *New York Times Magazine*, July 5, 2005, 30–32.

4. Stephen Metcalf, "Believing in Bullion," *New York Times Magazine*, June 5, 2005, 40.

5. Sharon Begley, "Scientific Proof That Money Isn't Everything," *Wall Street Journal Classroom Edition*, October 2004, 9.

6. Begley, "Scientific Proof," 9.

7. North American Precis Syndicate, "Teenagers Say 'Being Happy' Is the American Dream," *The Record*, Hackensack, NJ, March 6, 2005, J-5.

8. U.S. Census Bureau, "Income Stable, Poverty Rate Increases, Percentage of Americans without Health Insurance Unchanged," *U.S. Census Bureau News*, August 30, 2005 (accessed July 18, 2006).

2 Let's Call It Income: Allowance and Beyond

Does the word *allowance* suggest putting quarters in a piggy bank? In case you find the term outdated, irrelevant, or annoying, think *income* instead. In any case we're talking about the amount of money that you personally have to spend.

"I get a regular allowance."—Melissa, age 16

"I usually ask for money and tell them what it's for, and then they give it to me based on what I'm going to do with it."—Jake, age 17

"My mom just gives me $20 for lunch every day. I think I'm overpaid."—Keith, age 15

"I do not get an allowance, but sometimes when I need it my guardian gives it to me. I work, so they feel they should not have to give me money." —Vondae, age 16

WHO GETS ALLOWANCE?

According to a 2000 teen poll, teenagers "typically get money from their parents when they need it and occasionally earn money by doing odd jobs. Between one-fourth and one-third of teenagers receive a regular allowance or have a regular or part-time job."[1] The same poll shows that 97 percent of teens do

some chore or other to earn that allowance. *Zillions* magazine found that kids 13 and older are less likely to get a fixed allowance than those under 13.[2]

Kids who consider their families to be "middle income" report receiving about half of their spending money from parents or guardians.[3] Some, of course, expect no money at all. Phil, age 17, says, "My parents call what they give me a gift, and now that I work, I have to pay them off." If you're in the young adult majority, however, your parents probably give you a set amount every day, week, or month, or else they dole out money gradually for your necessities and extras.

HOW SHOULD ALLOWANCE BE PAID?

So, which is better—regular allowance or the irregular handout? The good aspects of a fixed allowance, from your point of view, are security—you can count on a certain amount and plan ahead; fewer hassles with parents—you don't have to keep negotiating constantly; and the chance to learn from your mistakes. Meanwhile, the worst aspect of a fixed allowance is that the designated amount may not be realistic. Surprise expenses are sure to crop up or regular expenses may fluctuate.

Whether you're better off, or worse off, with parents doling out money as you need it will probably depend on how generous they are and how good you are at convincing them. The downsides of collecting-as-you-go are that your income may depend on a parent's mood, you won't be able to plan ahead, your family will have more control over your spending, and you'll be deprived of the opportunity to budget for yourself.

There's also debate on whether kids should have to do chores in exchange for allowance. *The Complete Idiot's Guide to Money for Teens* says that although giving kids money for household chores is "a common practice in many homes, it's fallen out of favor among many financial advisors and family counselors."[4] The argument here is that teenagers should help around the house anyway, *without pay*, because they're part of the family.

HOW MUCH?

Let's cut to the bottom line—an expression that refers to the last line of a budget, where you see if you're "in the black" (you've got assets) or "in the red" (you're in debt). Assuming you receive some money from your family, how much should you expect? Certain advice books and websites aimed at parents suggest specific amounts or general guidelines (such as $1 a week for every year of your life), but systems like that ignore at least three things—big differences in family income; price differences depending on where you live; and inflation, which is the general rise in the level of prices over time.

No matter what experts say, the amount of money you get from your family will most likely depend on a combination of what your family can afford, your family's lifestyle, and your family's personal philosophy about kids and money. It's no surprise that most people your age would like to have more money, but believe it or not, the occasional young adult, such as Rex, age 17, says, "I get money as needed, sometimes perhaps too much. My mom is willing to give me $200 a month, even if I spend only maybe $75. 'Just in case,' she says." Another example of this rare problem is a teenage New York City girl, who—hurt by resentful remarks from friends and classmates— says, "I wish I didn't have so much!"[5]

Unfortunately there are too many examples of the opposite extreme—teens living in poverty. Statistics for 2004 showed 13 million such kids under 18.[6] Wherever you live, there are likely to be great variations in kids' incomes. Even those who live in the same town and go to the same school often have very different means. Expenses in metropolitan areas are greater than in small towns. Even in cities, though, there's a wide range, as evidenced by these voices of New York City teenagers:[7]

- **Steven, age 14:** "Every day I get $5, except Thursday and Friday because my dad doesn't work those days."
- **Dan, age 17:** "I get somewhere between $20 and $30 at the beginning of the week from my mom. . . . She'd probably give me more . . . but I hate taking money from her. I guess growing up in a single-parent home has made me want to be more self-reliant."
- **Julie, age 19:** "I put everything on the credit card and my parents pay the balance. There's no limit. . . . They don't even notice; it just all gets mixed up in their own charges."

NEGOTIATING ALLOWANCE

In most cases your parents or guardians hold the purse strings. Does that mean you're at their mercy, that you have to accept whatever arrangements they set up? Let's hope that in all matters, money included, your parents are reasonable and willing to communicate. If they aren't open to discussion, or, especially, if you know they can't afford to give you more, the best solution is to find ways to earn money yourself.

Let's say, though, that you're constantly broke and your parents *may* be willing to listen to you. When the right moment arrives (you're alone with your parents, they aren't in a big rush or in a bad mood, and you've just done something to earn brownie points) you make a calm, fact-based pitch, employing any of these strategies that apply:

- **Keep a written record of your spending for a couple of weeks and let the numbers tell the story. It may be a pain to be so organized, but numbers on paper make a much stronger**

BEFORE YOU NEGOTIATE,
ASK YOURSELF . . .

▶ **Can my family afford to give me a raise?**
▶ **Have I prepared a good case to persuade them?**
▶ **Can I make my pitch calmly?**
▶ **Is the timing right?**

impression than ones pulled out of the air. It would also be smart in that recording period to spend super-responsibly.

◎ Have a list in your head of additional reasons why you deserve a raise. For instance, you haven't gotten one for a while. You have new expenses. Prices have gone up. Maybe you'll offer to take on additional responsibilities around the house.

◎ At the risk of hearing your parents complain, "I don't care how much so-and-so gets!" find out what other kids are receiving. Tell it straight and pick as examples kids your parents know and respect.

◎ Be wary of comparing your income with that of your siblings, but if you can get mileage out of appealing for fairness, give it a try.

◎ If your parents are stuck back in the day when a movie cost $2, try showing them, by clicking on the Internet (CNNMoney.com), what a generous allowance in their time would be worth today.

Let's hope that one way or another you're in the 64 percent of teenagers who felt, as expressed in a *USA Weekend* poll, that they had enough money (as opposed to the 36 percent who said they never had enough).[8]

As a final word on the subject of your personal income, if you're satisfied, great. If you aren't—even after giving your best pitch—then you've got two choices: cut expenses or get a job. We'll talk further in upcoming chapters about saving money as

BUCK-SAVING TIPS

1. Carry membership and ID cards that may get you discounts at public and school events, restaurants, movies, and shows.
2. Look for freebies, clip coupons (or print them out from the Internet), send in rebates, and stay alert for sales.
3. With one or more friends, buy in large quantities things you use all the time, such as snacks, beverages, and computer and school supplies.
4. Instead of buying expensive presents, give something personal, original, or homemade. (Your friends may call it tacky, but adults will probably be touched.)
5. Instead of buying new, consider borrowing or trading with friends and buying at thrift shops and yard sales.

a consumer, and about jobs, but in the meantime have a look above at Buck-Saving Tips.

NOTES

1. As part of ICR's TeenEXCEL survey in February 2000, 515 boys and girls, ages 12–17, were interviewed. philanthropy.ml .com/ipo/resources/pdf/2000teen.pdf (accessed July 27, 2005).

2. Reported in Jayne A. Pearl, *Kids and Money* (Princeton, NJ: Bloomberg Press, 1999), 14.

3. Surveys were given to 193,224 students, grades 6–12. "Special Report: Teens & Money," *USA Weekend*, May 2, 1999, www.usaweekend.com/99_issues/990502/990502surveyresults.html (accessed September 5, 2004).

4. Susan Shelly, *The Complete Idiot's Guide to Money for Teens* (Indianapolis, IN: Alpha Books, 2001), 43–44.

5. David Amsden, "The Teenage Economy," *New York*, January 17, 2005, 18.

6. U.S. Census Bureau, "Poverty: 2004 Highlights," n.d., www.census.gov/hhes/www/poverty/poverty04/pov04hi.html (accessed January 17, 2006).

7. Amsden, "The Teenage Economy," 21.

8. "Special Report: Teens & Money," *USA Weekend*, 2.

3 Landing a Job: An Earning Experience

You're broke. Your parents can't, or won't, increase what they give you. Or maybe they need a contribution from you. Gift money isn't happening. It's time to think about getting a job. Or else you already have one but the rewards could be better. If you haven't yet worked for money outside your house, consider the pros and cons. The obvious good points are that a job gives you money to spend, save, or contribute to the family. You may also meet new people, gain experience for future jobs, and develop a feeling of independence.

> "I work as a receptionist at my church for extra money. I like it because it is not very busy, so I get to do homework."—Elena, age 15
>
> "I earn money working full-time at Walgreen's as a cosmetician. I really hate working. It's stressful and tiring. It's hard to balance eight hours in school and seven hours at work. Sometimes I feel that my mother doesn't understand how difficult it is. But I can't quit because now I'm expected to buy things for myself and the household."—Phylecia, age 16

DOWNSIDE OF A JOB

On the other hand, a job will eat into your free time and possibly add stress to your life. Getting to work may be a

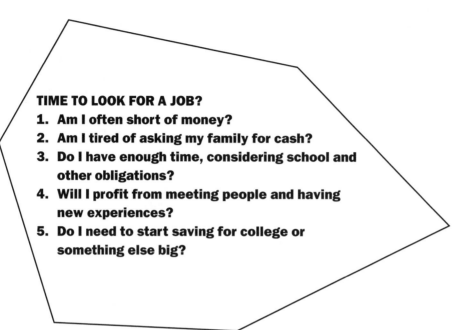

TIME TO LOOK FOR A JOB?
1. **Am I often short of money?**
2. **Am I tired of asking my family for cash?**
3. **Do I have enough time, considering school and other obligations?**
4. **Will I profit from meeting people and having new experiences?**
5. **Do I need to start saving for college or something else big?**

problem. And don't forget that certain job-related expenses may affect your profits, such as transportation, clothing, and tax deductions.

Advice in *The Complete Idiot's Guide to Money for Teens* is, "If you do get a job, you'll have to learn to prioritize. That means doing what absolutely has to be done first, and leaving optional activities for later." This guide emphasizes the importance of organizing your time, committing yourself to the job, and discussing the practicalities with parents or guardians before you start looking for work.[1] It should be no surprise that in a Lexington, Kentucky, poll 54 percent of working teenagers found "being tired" the toughest aspect of holding a job.[2]

Will commitment to a job cause your schoolwork to suffer? Some experts believe that working more than 20 hours per week may adversely affect your schoolwork. One study, for instance, indicates that students with heavy work schedules missed more school, reported more physical and psychological problems, and had higher rates of alcohol and drug use.[3] Other researchers, however, claim that time spent working is well worth it because it contributes to your overall development and some part-time jobs lead to lifetime careers.

HOW MANY KIDS WORK AND FOR HOW MUCH?

If you do take a job, you'll have a lot of teenage company. U.S. Department of Labor statistics show that more than 7 million young adults, ages 16 to 19, held jobs at some point in 2003.[4] By the time they graduate from high school, 80 percent of U.S. teenagers have been employed, at least on a part-time basis.[5] The exact percentage and numbers are hard to pin down though, because some kids work full-time, most work part-time, and some work only seasonally.

What kinds of jobs are these kids holding? A majority of working teens have jobs in retail stores and restaurants, and just under one-quarter work in the service sector, which includes entertainment, recreation, domestic labor, and health care. Remaining teenage workers are distributed among farming, manufacturing, and other industries.[6]

Teens who hold these jobs aren't likely to get rich. "Fewer than 10 percent earned more than $5,000 in a 1997–1998 survey." Most kids work for spending money, not to support themselves or to help their families, and most teen earnings go to personal expenses such as clothing and entertainment.[7] Researcher Jerald G. Bachman believes that some teenagers may experience "premature affluence." That is, if you earn a fair amount of money from a part-time job while living at home, you may get used to spending freely and be unprepared for supporting yourself once you're on your own.[8]

One way to avoid premature affluence is to volunteer for a job, without pay. Volunteering may be smart in the long run because it provides experience that may lead to a paid position. Volunteering will also look good on your record and may make you feel good about yourself.

TYPES OF JOBS

Let's say, though, that you've decided you want to earn money. What kind of job should you try for, and how do you go about looking? If you're like Christian, age 17, you won't even have to look. He says, "All jobs I had were through family. I've worked at my uncle's hair salon and more recently with my

dad who's in construction." A family business or family
connection gives you an obvious leg-up in getting employed.
On the other hand, if you prefer to work for someone outside
your family, you can try to make your own arrangements for a
typical freelance job, such as babysitting or grass cutting, or
pursue a formal job with a company or an organization.
Maybe you'll be attracted by one of the many "Now Hiring"
banners regularly on display at well-known chain stores and
restaurants.

If you work at a fast-food restaurant or a shop in the mall, you'll be in the profit-making sector, and if you work as a health aide, library assistant, or helper in a religious institution, you'll be in the nonprofit world. You may earn less money working for a nonprofit group, but if you enjoy the job and feel good about it, the amount of the paycheck may not matter that much. Even if you work for a profit-making organization, as an inexperienced worker you may be paid the minimum wage.

Keep your eyes open for part-time jobs.

STEPS IN LOOKING FOR A JOB

Once you decide to look for a job, unless you've already gone through the process, you'll need to learn the drill, which will probably include the following:

1. Networking
2. Checking out help-wanted ads
3. Signing up with a career center or employment agency
4. Writing a résumé
5. Sending out applications
6. Attending interviews
7. Taking tests

How to get started? Networking. It's great if a relative drops a job in your lap, but if you have to take the initiative, try networking as a first step. According to Jayne A. Pearl, in *Kids and Money*, "The majority of jobs are never advertised or listed. The best way to tap this 'hidden job market' is by word of mouth."[9] "At any given time, about 80% of all available jobs aren't posted in the classifieds or on job boards . . . and 60% of people surveyed said they got their last job by networking."[10] Networking means asking if you and your family know anybody who could give you a lead on a job. It might be a family friend; a professional, such as your family's doctor, dentist, or vet; a teacher at school; or one of your own friends who already works. By the way, it's usually smart to ask this person for advice, instead of asking directly for a job.

Your first lucky break will come if networking produces a job, and your second break will be if the available job is a good fit for you. It goes without saying that it's better to do something for money that you're actually good at and enjoy, so you may as well try for the ideal before settling for less. *Teen Dream Jobs: How to Find the Job You Really Want Now!* by teen author Nora E. Coon, includes interviews with young adults who have been successful DJs, musicians, models, chocolatiers, and beekeepers.[11] The possibilities for self-created freelance jobs are endless. Sheriffa, age 16, makes money braiding hair; Paul, age 18, videotapes events for his clients; and Avram, age 17, plays gigs at an off-Broadway children's show. Chances are, getting a glamorous job is going to be as rare as drawing a winning lottery ticket, so you may end up taking a starting position that isn't your ideal.

What next, if networking doesn't pan out? Help-wanted ads and employment agencies. The most obvious sources of ads are your local newspapers, including giveaway papers; your school's guidance staff and/or job center, if one exists; and job listings online. *The Complete Idiot's Guide to Cool Jobs for Teens* urges kids to check the classified section every day, to watch for help-wanted signs in storefront windows, to look in the Yellow Pages for names of employment agencies, and to go to your state employment agency's website or visit its actual office.[12] Most websites are geared to adults looking for full-time positions, but some sites list jobs appropriate for teenagers. If you go online looking for a job, be prepared to be the recipient of endless e-mail.

Check help-wanted ads in local newspapers.

How do you introduce yourself to employers? Through résumés, which are one- or two-page summaries of your education, training, experience, and job qualifications. A chronological résumé lists your education, work experience, and related information year by year. A skills, or functional, résumé emphasizes your abilities in specific categories. The skills résumé usually makes more sense for young adults looking for part-time jobs. Along with a résumé send a cover letter that tells why you're interested in a certain job and why you would be good at it. You may get part-time or summer work without ever being asked for a résumé, but at some point in your life you'll probably have to create one. Nice-guy employers will acknowledge your résumé even if they can't use you. On the other hand, you may send out résumés and not get a response.

When you write a résumé or a cover letter, be clear about the job you're interested in, tell how you learned about it, and explain why you believe you're qualified. In addition, don't lie. Follow a model from a reliable book on résumé-writing. Be brief, organize well, and use word processing software. Have a responsible person proofread and save everything you write in a computer.

What will most potential employers want from you? A job application. Where do you get it? Either you're given one by an employer or else you take the initiative. You can go directly to a place of business or telephone or e-mail them. Filling out job applications is usually straightforward, but if you're new to the scene, consider the following points:

- If you don't already have a Social Security number (SSN), apply for one by picking up a form at your local Social Security office (look in the phone book), by calling the federal Social Security office (1-800-772-1213), or by going online to www.ssa.gov/online/ss-5.html, where you can download the form. (The current practice of the Social Security service of having mothers apply for SSNs for babies at the time of their birth will make it unnecessary in the future for teenagers to apply.)

- If you have more than one address and/or phone number, give both.

- If you're asked what salary you expect, write "minimum wage," unless you know you have special skills or you have already earned more on a previous job.

- If you're asked whether it's okay to contact a current employer, answer on the basis of whether you want your boss to know that you're looking for another job.

- If you have never had a formal job and are asked to list previous employers, leave a blank if you must, or else list relevant odd jobs.

- If you're asked why you left a previous job and the reason is a problem (let's say you were fired), don't lie, but choose your words carefully ("needed to move on").

- Prepare ahead for references. Ask in advance if you may use the names (with addresses and phone numbers) of a teacher who likes you, a former employer, a coach or other activity sponsor, a religious leader, or a respected friend of your family.

- Think about which adult you will list under "In case of emergency."

- Be straightforward about your age.

> ⊚ **If you're asked whether you've been convicted of a crime (or felony), you must by law say yes if the crime is serious. You don't need to mention a minor parking offense.**

When do employers meet you face to face? In an interview. How do you dress? Neatly and in keeping with the requirements of the job. Avoid extremes such as low-cut tops for females and low-slung jeans for males. In fact, avoid jeans altogether, even if the job itself involves physical labor. If possible, consult an informed person about what dress code, if any, is favored by the employer.

What else is there to know? Find out, in advance, other information about the company and the interviewer. Carry a pen, notepad, and copy of your résumé. Be friendly, smile, and offer the interviewer a handshake. Make eye contact, watch your posture, and avoid chewing gum. Finally, be honest and speak distinctly.[13]

Another suggestion before going to an interview is to prepare an "elevator speech." That is, write a summary of what you want a prospective employer to know about you—who you are, what you do, what you're looking for. Practice this 30-second speech in front of a mirror so that you're comfortable introducing yourself at an interview.[14] There are other ways to practice interviewing. Childhood friends Miles Munz and Randy Biting won an award in 2003 for a product called RezFusion, a computerized kiosk in career centers that enables job seekers to participate in virtual interviews.[15] One more suggestion: before your interview, come up with a list of things you want to know about the job, and if any points aren't covered by the interviewer, make sure to ask. Am I likely to get tips? Is there an employee discount? Employee benefits?

TALKING YOURSELF INTO A JOB

An additional point about the way you talk: "Humphrey S. Tyler, president of National Trade Publications, frequently rejects sales and editorial candidates because they exhibit grammatically incorrect speech. 'It's as if they pulled out a baseball cap and put it on backward.'"[16] Interviewees have also been criticized for "uptalk," a singsong pattern, often heard from teenagers, a pattern in which the speaker of a statement makes it sound like a question. A result is that speakers of uptalk may come off as uncertain and lacking in confidence. If you're aware of having this habit, you might try to play it down. Changing speech is a big challenge but is usually worth the effort.

SMOKING YOURSELF OUT OF A JOB

Another challenge for job-seeking smokers is to quit the habit in order to be considered for employment by companies such as Weyco of Okemos, Michigan, and Investors Property Management in Seattle, Washington, where they hire nonsmokers only. The latter company is considering requiring a blood test as proof.[17] Even more companies are likely to reject smokers in the future if costs of medical insurance continue to rise.

BEWARE OF DANGER

With decent speech, plus determination and luck, you'll be in a favorable position to join the teenage majority—those who have work experience. Be wary, of course, of taking a dangerous job. "According to the National Institute for Occupational Safety and Health, 73 teens under age 18 were killed on the job in 2000—and 29 of them were under the age of 16. An average of 231,000 teenagers under the age of 18 are injured on the job each year."[18] According to a list published by the National Consumers League in 2004, the five worst teen jobs are

1. **agriculture, where the rate of fatal injuries to workers 15–17 is higher than in most other workplaces.**
2. **working alone and late-night work in retail, where deaths and injuries are mostly robbery related.**
3. **construction, which has the third highest rate of fatalities, usually caused by falling from roofs or ladders.**
4. **driving or operating forklifts or tractors.**
5. **door-to-door selling of magazine subscriptions or other merchandise in high-crime neighborhoods.[19]**

The federal government, since 1938, has been watching out for you. Before that, kids were often exploited. The Fair Labor Standards Act (FLSA), which includes child labor laws, sets minimum age, wages, and conditions for workers under 18. The state you live in may have additional restrictions (concerning, for instance, the age at which you're allowed to serve alcoholic beverages). To keep up-to-date on laws affecting your work, check the website YouthRules! established by the U.S. Department of Labor in 2002.

If you want a really safe job—that is, working out of your own house—some Internet organizations offer to pay you in money or reward points for giving your opinions on issues, products, media, and services. Be cautious of these arrangements though, especially if you're asked to give personal information about yourself or your parents. An online polling organization may take advantage of the data you provide. If you decide to respond to opinion polls or anything else on the Internet, get an okay from a parent or guardian, whether the website requires it or not.

Other jobs to avoid are ones that sound unbelievably easy or too well paid. For instance, some Internet and magazine ads promise you hundreds of dollars a month for conducting sales from your house. Avoid illegal activities. Selling illegal substances and/or hot merchandise can obviously land you in serious trouble. Other unethical projects can jeopardize your future. For example, for the price of $1,000, an academically talented senior attending an independent school in New Jersey in 2003 took the Scholastic Aptitude Test in place of another student. The pretender was recognized by a proctor at the test site and was expelled from high school. Not too smart.

GOOD TO BE YOUNG?

So how tough is it going to be to get a safe, legal, decent-paying job? Is your age going to be held against you? Let's face it. Even though there are federal laws preventing employers from discriminating against a person on the basis of age, race, color, religion, gender, marital status, national origin, or mental or physical disabilities, you may lose out when competing against someone older and more experienced. In fast foods and other young-adult-dominated areas, however, your youth may be an advantage. If you happen to get a job where you're the youngest worker, you may as well be prepared for what Adrena, age 16, found. "I was fairly paid but sometimes at my daycare job they would make me do certain jobs that the older workers didn't do."

PAYCHECKS

Speaking of salary—is an employer allowed to pay you peanuts? No. Fortunately, one of the protections offered by the FLSA is a guaranteed minimum wage, for most jobs. As of early 2007, Congress was on its way to raising the minimum wage from $5.15 per hour to $7.25 per hour. More than half the states already have a minimum wage that is higher than $5.15 per hour. (The highest state minimum wages are currently in the high $7-per-hour range.[20])

Remember, though, that at the same time the federal government is protecting you, it's also taking its cut. Once you're on a payroll, be prepared to deal with the following taxes deducted from your paycheck: (1) federal income, (2) Social Security (FICA), (3) Medicare, and (4) state income (in most states). These deductions may seem unfair, but if you and other workers didn't pay them, there wouldn't be any reasonable way to fund schools, roads, defense of the country, and many other services.

The good news is that if you earn less than $4,400 in a year, you'll get a refund of the federal taxes you paid. If you earn between $4,400 and $23,350, you'll pay 15 percent of your earnings—money you won't get back. And if you're lucky enough to earn more than $23,350 in a year, maybe you won't mind so much that the tax rate goes up to 28 percent.

SAVING FOR LATER

Here's another great scenario. You're doing well on your job and you don't need every penny you make to support your present lifestyle. Think about putting some of your earnings into an IRA (Individual Retirement Account). This is a retirement savings plan that allows you to postpone paying some of your taxes. For more information on IRAs see chapters 6 and 15.

BEING YOUR OWN BOSS

Now let's consider an alternative route to making money. You'd like to be your own boss, run your own business. Brittany, age 17, says, "I bought a large supply of candy and then sold individual pieces for more than I paid. I'm trying to learn to make my own candy." Brittany's just one of many teenagers who, motivated by their own ambition, by TV shows like *The Apprentice*, by school organizations like JumpStart!, and by websites like YoungBiz.com, decide to bypass ordinary jobs and literally go for broke. Plenty of kids go through a lemonade-stand phase, but few have the determination, smarts, and luck to become successful entrepreneurs.

Here are some teenage entrepreneurs who have beaten the odds:

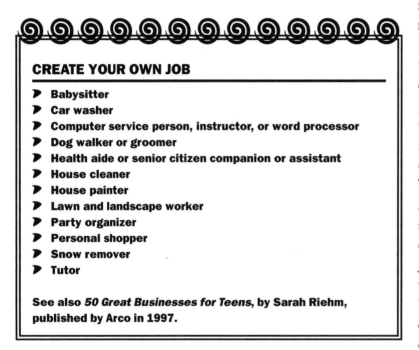

CREATE YOUR OWN JOB

- ▶ Babysitter
- ▶ Car washer
- ▶ Computer service person, instructor, or word processor
- ▶ Dog walker or groomer
- ▶ Health aide or senior citizen companion or assistant
- ▶ House cleaner
- ▶ House painter
- ▶ Lawn and landscape worker
- ▶ Party organizer
- ▶ Personal shopper
- ▶ Snow remover
- ▶ Tutor

See also *50 Great Businesses for Teens*, by Sarah Riehm, published by Arco in 1997.

◎ Camille Winbush, of Pasadena, California, made $120,000 in her first year of running a parlor that specializes in homemade-cookie ice-cream sandwiches. Camille, who was earning money as an actor since age 2, had the advantage of more start-up funds than most kids, which helped her, at age 13, to launch a business called Baked Ice.

⊚ Rich Stachowski, of Orinda, California, has made a fortune and gotten a lot of publicity from selling to a toy manufacturer the underwater walkie-talkie he invented.

⊚ Can you believe this? Two friends in Stillwater, Oklahoma, Coy Funk and Skylar Schipper, have made serious money and a big reputation from their business, Manure Gourmet. They collect dung from sheep, goats, and llamas, sun-dry it into odorless manure, and market it on the Internet.[21]

⊚ Akailah Watkins is cofounder and codirector of I AM (Imagine, Accept, and Materialize), a nonprofit company dedicated to helping kids start their own businesses. She began her operation with money she collected from selling salvaged furniture at garage sales, she employed kids who were hanging out on the streets, and she brought in $150,000 in 2004.[22]

⊚ While he was still in high school, Michael Simmons of Hopewell, New Jersey, and his friend Calvin Newport formed a Web-development company called Princeton Web Solutions, which brought in an income of $30,000 a month. Later, in business school at New York University, Michael wrote an eBook, *The Student Success Manifesto*, that tells about his experiences and gives advice to would-be entrepreneurs.[23]

Successful business owners, young or old, usually have a great need to achieve, to escape from traditional jobs, and to be their own boss. The benefits of running your own business are obvious: no time clock, no one telling you what to do, profits in your own pocket, and the chance to meet people and become well-known. The downside, though, even if you turn a profit, includes long hours, tough decision making, financial and legal risks, and stress.

The thing to remember about any regular job or business of your own is that in addition to the money you make, you're gaining experience.

NOTES

1. Susan Shelly, *The Complete Idiot's Guide to Money for Teens* (Indianapolis, IN: Alpha Books, 2001), 61–62.

2. Mary Meehan, "Teens at Work Tired but Satisfied," April 20, 2004, www.sunherald.com/mld/sunherald/8471664 .htm?template=Modules/printst, 1 (accessed October 30, 2004).

3. Lynn Slaughter, "Should Your Teen Work during the School Year?" *Harford County KiDS Magazine*, August 2002, www.harfordcountykids.com/department.cfm?id=3, 1 (accessed May 17, 2005).

4. U.S. Department of Labor, "Tomorrow's Jobs," Bureau of Labor Statistics Data, 2003, www.bls.gov/oco/oco2003.htm (accessed June 19, 2005).

5. Julian Barling and E. Kevin Kelloway, *Young Workers: Varieties of Experience* (Washington, DC: American Psychological Association, 1999).

6. Alison Morantz, "Teens in the Workforce," *Regional Review*, Quarter 2, 2001, www.bos.frb.org/economic/nerr/rr2001/q2/teens .htm, 2 (accessed May 17, 2005).

7. Morantz, "Teens in the Workforce," 3.

8. Jerald G. Bachman, "Premature Affluence: Do High School Students Earn Too Much?" *Economic Outlook USA*, Summer 1983.

9. Jayne A. Pearl, *Kids and Money* (Princeton, NJ: Bloomberg Press, 1999), 196.

10. Stacey L. Bradford, "Networking Opens Door for Job Hunters," *Wall Street Journal Classroom Edition*, April 2005, 5.

11. Nora E. Coon, *Teen Dream Jobs: How to Find the Job You Really Want Now!* (Hillsboro, OR: Beyond Words Publishing, 2001).

12. Susan Ireland, *The Complete Idiot's Guide to Cool Jobs for Teens* (Indianapolis, IN: Alpha Books), 130–32.

13. Ireland, *Complete Idiot's Guide to Cool Jobs*, 174–75.

14. Bradford, "Networking Opens Door for Job Hunters," 5.

15. Lauren Berger, "Job Interviews Go High Tech," *Young Money*, September/October 2004, 12.

16. Joanne Lublin, "Watch What You Say, And How You Say It," *Wall Street Journal Classroom Edition*, December 2004, 5.

17. Kris Maher, "Smokers Need Not Apply," *Wall Street Journal Classroom Edition*, March 2005, 4.

18. Neale S. Godfrey, *Money Still Doesn't Grow on Trees* (Emmaus, PA: Rodale, 2004), 158.

19. Carol McKay, "Teen Workers: Beware These Five Worst Summer '04 Jobs," National Consumers League, n.d., www.nclnet .org/pressroom/teenjobs04.htm (accessed January 2, 2007).

20. U.S. Department of Labor, "Minimum Wage Laws in the States—January 1, 2007," *Employment Standards Administration, Wage and Hour Division*, December 2006, www.dol.gov/esa/minwage/america.htm (accessed January 30, 2007).

21. The entrepreneurship of Winbush, Stachowski, and Funk and Schipper is described in *People*, November 8, 2004, 127–29.

22. Tonia L. Shakespeare, "5 Great Businesses for Young Entrepreneurs," December 1996, www.allbusiness.com/specialty-businesses/minority-owned-businesses/583901-1.html (accessed January 2, 2007).

23. Kate Tobin, "NYU Student Writes Book for Entrepreneur Hopefuls," 2003, www.youngmoney.com/entrepreneur/entrepreneur_profiles/071603_01 (accessed January 2, 2007).

4 Shaking the Money Tree: Windfalls

MONEY GIFTS

Is there any hope of income beyond what you get from your family and part-time job? Whatever extra comes your way is probably unpredictable. Maybe you have generous grandparents. If your relatives give you presents instead of money, is there anything wrong with letting them know you'd like money instead? It depends. Some people think money gifts are impersonal or even rude, and others are happy that they don't have to shop. If you sense that your family is against money gifts, forget asking for them. If you sense that they won't be offended, drop a few hints.

Is it possible that you have hidden assets—money that's yours but you don't know about it? It's not unusual for parents to forget about a savings account or bond that a relative bought in your name when you were born. Chances are, if there is such an asset, it won't be yours to spend now, but knowing that you have a nest egg can make you feel good.

GAMBLING

Let's talk about real windfalls—winning at gambling. Can you seriously boost your income by relying on luck? "Just the other day, with family members, I bought three scratch-off cards in the State Lottery," says Andrea, age 19. "One was for $50! At a West Virginia race track I once won $120." First of all, until you're 18, in most states you aren't eligible to participate in state-run gambling.[1] Second, even if you're over 18, odds are, you'll eventually be echoing Andrea, who admits, "Of course I've lost, too."

Getting hooked on lotteries is a terrible habit. "While casinos keep, on average, about 5 percent of every dollar you gamble, lotteries keep about *50 percent*, ten times more! . . . Many lottery players just buy a ticket every now and then . . . but more than 80 percent of all ticket sales come from just 20 percent of all the players. They spend more than $4 per day on tickets, more than $1,500 per year."[2]

Andrea, buying the occasional lottery ticket, isn't the person the National Academy of Sciences is worrying about. This organization is alarmed, however, about the growing number of young problem gamblers, many of them caught up in poker—actual games and those on TV. "Almost one in three high school students gambles on a regular basis."[3]

Do you see yourself as someone who could get hooked on gambling? Researchers find that adolescents who gamble often don't realize that they have a problem, and the possibility of becoming addicted to gambling is twice as great for teenage gamblers as for adults.[4]

People who see money as a way to be free and adventurous are most likely to gamble. Gambling can take many forms—playing the lottery, going to casinos, day trading stocks on the Internet, or choosing a job that pays on commission. A lot of people gamble because they aren't patient enough to work and save. If more kids today are gambling it's probably because access is easier than ever. "Sports betting is a major problem, and it's getting worse," says Ed Looney of the Council on Compulsive Gambling of New Jersey, Inc. And the easiest gambling access of all for young adults is the Internet. "Internet gambling has increased from one site to 1,400 in the past six years."[5]

Okay, everybody knows the odds are against you, but does *any* gambler end up winning? If you search the Internet looking for successful gamblers, you'll come up with more than a million and a half hits. But instead of accounts of happy people who won big, you'll find references to books that claim to teach you how to win, ads inviting you to gamble, and hotlines and groups offering help to gambling addicts.

"I TOOK MONEY OUT OF MY MOM'S PURSE . . ."[6]

"I gambled as a teenager," says Karen H. "I learned how to shoot dice, and I shot dice with the boys at my junior high school. It was just the excitement. I took money out of my mom's purse to gamble."

Daughter of alcoholics, Karen continued gambling after her marriage until she had children and eventually joined Gamblers Anonymous. Free of gambling now for 24 years and executive secretary of Gamblers Anonymous International Service Office in Los Angeles, California, Karen says, "I realized I could have a better way of life. I do it one day at a time."

Not that scary stories are likely to keep you away from that football pool or Texas Hold'em session, but here's some disturbing information anyway: problem gambling in adolescence often goes hand in hand with poorer school performance, lower self-esteem, higher rates of depression, increased risk of developing other addictions, increased chance of delinquency, and heightened risk for suicidal thoughts and suicide attempts.[7]

And if that's not enough, this is what just one survey showed about 98 serious problem gamblers in a Wisconsin Gamblers Anonymous group: They averaged nearly $100,000 losses during their gambling careers. One-third of them stole money. Twenty-one percent lost or quit their jobs. Eleven had been in jail. Seventy percent of those who were divorced or separated blamed the breakup on gambling.[8]

A safe conclusion is, if you want to be rich and also happy, find an occupation other than gambling. Remember, though, that if you or anyone you know is a problem gambler, there are a growing number of groups, like Gamblers Anonymous, that offer help.

CONTEST PRIZES

The difference is obvious between buying a lottery ticket and entering a contest with a money prize. A lottery is based on pure luck, but a contest usually rewards a skill or favorable attribute. In either case the chances of winning may be slim, but contests can be fun, and unless they're completely rigged, you have a chance. Most contests sponsored by, or publicized in, schools and other reputable institutions are what they claim to be and have no hidden agenda. For instance, if you're an artist or writer, submit your work to the annual Scholastic Art and Writing Awards. If you're science oriented, find out about the Siemens Westinghouse Competition, and if you're interested in business, pursue the Jumpstart 250 Awards. Oprah Winfrey, in January 2006, initiated a teen essay contest with scholarships and guest appearances on her show as prizes. Ask teachers about these contests or get more information from websites.

If you see an ad for an unfamiliar contest, however, proceed with caution. A lot of these contests, even if legitimate, are hooks to grab customers. The sponsors may want, in exchange for a shot at prize money, information about you and your family, so that they can eventually sell you something or get you interested in their beliefs. (Some contests are sponsored by religious or political groups.) Another point: if you search the Internet for "contests with money prizes for teenagers," you'll find so many possibilities that you'd make more money putting that same amount of time into a job. These contests range from fun, interesting, and educational to silly, misleading, and exploitative.

Be especially wary of contests that offer money prizes for your poetry. Watch out, also, for those who promise to publish your poems in a book. The only way you'll get to see your published poetry is by buying the expensive volumes that make a big profit for these so-called contest sponsors. By the calculations of one "winner," Theresa Coleman, a company called the International Library of Poetry makes about $14 million per year from books and conventions that take advantage of would-be poets who enter their contests.[9]

FREE POETRY CONTEST
$100,000 IN PRIZES AWARDED ANNUALLY
ONLINE ENTRY FORM

Angela A.	David F.	Jeff and Brenda C.	Vicki C.	Sophie L.
Philadelphia, Penn.	Cape Town, S. Africa	Rockwall, Texas	Fort Myers, Florida	San Francisco, Calif.
$1,000 Prize Winner	$10,000 Prize Winner	$10,000 Prize Winner	$10,000 Prize Winner	$10,000 Prize Winner

Submit a poem below and you could be our next winner!

NEXT $1000 WINNER   9/15/2006
NEXT $10,000 WINNER   1/15/2007
FREE entry form! Bookmark this page!

Poetry.com will award 1175 prizes totaling **$100,000.00** to amateur poets in the coming months. Type your name, street address, and poem below and then click submit!

Anyone can enter the competition simply by submitting an original poem, 20 lines or fewer with a maximum of 60 characters per line, on any subject, in any style. If your poem makes it to the semi-finals, you will receive an acknowledgment by regular mail within seven weeks.

First: Middle: Last:

Email Address:

Be wary of contests that claim you'll win big bucks.

Also beware of deals like this one. Jack McCall of New York was happy to hear he'd won a video-making contest sponsored by American Airlines. His grand prize, valued at $52,800, was 12 round-trip coach tickets for two from the United States to anywhere American flies. Unfortunately Jack had to turn down the prize after he calculated the federal and state income taxes on his prize. Taxes would have amounted to $19,000.[10]

An outright scam, worse than a poetry contest or a taxed flight around the world, is the telephone call to your family announcing that you've won a free cruise. The caller may ask for a small amount of money, or a credit card number, to confirm the prize. Any contest that asks you to pay money is prohibited by law. And giving out your credit card number may result in someone's "borrowing" your card.[11]

In the silly-but-harmless category, Steven Cullen and his prom date competed for scholarship money given by a duct tape manufacturer. The first prize, offered on the Internet by stuckonprom.com, was $5,000. The two kids fashioned prom wear out of rolls of colored duct tape, at a cost they figured to be about the same as buying a dress and renting a tux.[12]

A more typical Internet contest offer can be found on a site like Next Step, a teen magazine publisher, which offers a few $5,000 and $1,000 scholarships; $100 money prizes for original writing; and other prizes such as books, laundry bags, and inflatable chairs. In order to be eligible you'll be asked for some required and some optional information, including your gender, ethnicity, PSAT and SAT scores, and grade point average. They will want you to check off a list that reflects your interests in careers, colleges, student loans, and "other stuff." Next Step makes it clear that it's offering money and scholarships in the hope that college-bound teenagers will buy certain products and use certain services.[13] Even if you don't win prizes, sites like these may provide helpful information.

And even if it's tough to win money in contests, you can get free items of all kinds. Free booklets, samples, and services are listed in sources such as *The Bottom Line Book of Freebies*, *Freebies* magazine, and *1001 Government Freebies and Cheapies*.[14]

SCHOLARSHIPS

Are you missing out on scholarship money? More than $4 billion a year is given out in the form of grants and loans, yet only 10 percent of those eligible actually apply. Many scholarships are awarded not on your need or your academic record alone but on the basis of community involvement, writing skills, and membership in particular associations.[15] Determining whether you're eligible takes a lot of time, effort, and know-how, so get all the help you can from parents, guardians, guidance counselors, school administrators, and teachers. The Internet is loaded with financial aid information at sites such as FastWeb and Scholarship Resources Network. ScholarshipExperts.com is an online service that charges a membership fee to help you locate appropriate scholarships, and AllScholar.com offers the same service without a fee.

BARTERING

Your total income from allowance, job, and windfalls leaves
you still feeling needy. Is there anything else you can do? Think
about bartering. This practice of swapping one thing for
another goes far back in history. Cattle, sheep, and goats were
traded in biblical times. Once human beings stopped roaming
and settled down, they often exchanged grain, vegetables,
pottery, or furniture for other goods or services. You may
already be routinely trading clothes, CDs, and other stuff with
friends. The same sort of exchange among strangers is the age-
old practice of barter—a way to get what you want without
spending precious bucks. Items to swap may include equipment
and clothing you've outgrown or lost interest in. Notices posted
in schools, supermarkets, and on residential and public bulletin
boards may help you exchange items. Ads in free newspapers
may also bring results. But, these days, the serious barterer will
probably go to the Internet.

You may already be familiar with eBay, "The World's Online
Marketplace," which claims to offer an online platform where
millions of items—electronics, furniture, art objects, just about
anything—are traded, not this for that, but are bought and sold
each day. A possible hitch here is that eBay says you are eligible
to become a member only if you are 18 or older. A parent or
guardian can, of course, act on your behalf until you reach the
minimum age, as in the case of Bradley Ziegler, 15, of Bergen
County, New Jersey. With the approval of his parents, Bradley
buys marked-down DVDs and GameCube games to resell on
eBay for as much as 10 times more than he paid.[16] For
information on how to buy or sell on eBay, go to its website.

Chris Pullen and Chip Davis, two enterprising St. Joseph,
Missouri, teens looking for fortune and adventure, offered
themselves in an eBay transaction. "Buy us for one week to do
those tedious tasks you hate!" they advertised.[17]

Other nonprofit community groups around the country also
arrange barters. For instance, the Pillsbury Neighborhood
Services' Community Barter Network in Minneapolis makes it
possible for teenagers to do chores in exchange for points that

can be used for "an impressive variety of services."[18] Leah Chapple Stingley, on Youth Radio, described another similar organization called BREAD (Berkeley Regional Exchange), whose members swap services and goods. "I know it sounds like a hippie commune that I wouldn't dare enter," she says, "but teenagers have always had a subculture of bartering."[19]

If you're tempted to deal with bartering groups on the Internet, it's a good idea to check their reliability by looking up "About Us" on their own website and, better yet, by seeing if they're listed on BBBOnLine (Better Business Bureau). The importance of this respected watchdog organization will come up more than once when we talk about giving to charity and being a consumer.

So—allowance, a job, occasional gifts, and exchanges. After you total up your resources, the next question is, What am I going to do with the money? Read on.

NOTES

1. Can you get into trouble buying a lottery ticket if you're under 18? Usually the person who sells the ticket is at greater risk. Some states make spot checks of vendors, but law and policies are hard to enforce.

2. David and Tom Gardner, *The Motley Fool Investment Guide for Teens* (New York: Fireside, 2002), 83–84; original emphasis.

3. PBS, "As More Teens Gamble, Experts Urge Public Education," *NewsHour Extra*, April 24, 2005, www.pbs.org/newshour/extra/features/jan-june05/gambling_4-25.html, 1 (accessed July 18, 2005).

4. Jeff Derevensky and Rina Gupta, "Youth Gambling: A Clinical and Research Perspective," *eGambling*, August 2000, www.camh.net/egambling/issue2/feature/ (accessed July 19, 2005).

5. April Spurlock, "Gambling Becoming Addiction among Teenagers, Young Adults," *Daily O'Collegian*, n.d., www.youngmoney.com/money_management/spending/020809_04, 1 (accessed July 18, 2005).

6. Laura Paul, "High Stakes: Teens Gambling with Their Futures," *Teenagers Today*, n.d., teenagerstoday.com/resources/articles/highstakes.htm, 1 (accessed March 5, 2005).

7. Derevensky and Gupta, "Youth Gambling," 4–5.

8. William N. Thompson, Ricardo Gazel, and Dan Rickman, "The Social Costs of Gambling in Wisconsin," Wisconsin Policy Research Institute Report, July 1996, www.casinowatch.org/loss_limit/wisconsin_report.html (accessed July 19, 2005).

9. Theresa Coleman, "Big Money in Poetry," Wind Publications, 2000, www.windpub.com/literary.scams/bigmoney.htm (accessed July 22, 2005).

10. Melanie Trottman and Ron Lieber, "Why Would You Turn Down a $52,000 Prize?" *Wall Street Journal Classroom Edition*, October 2005, 5.

11. "Telemarketing Scams," n.d., www.atg.wa.gov/teenconsumer/buying_goods_and_services/telemarketing_scams.htm (accessed January 2, 2007).

12. Nancy Green, "Sticking Together: Teens Try for Scholarship with Duct-Tape Prom Formals," *Star-Herald*, Kosciusko, MI, n.d., p&e@starherald.net (accessed July 20, 2005).

13. For more information on these scholarships and contests, check out the Next Step website at www.nextstepmagazine.com/nextstep/default.aspx.

14. Bottom Line Books, *The Bottom Line of Freebies* (Greenwich, CT: Bottom Line Books, 2003); *Freebies* magazine, www.freebies.com/; Matthew Lesko, *1001 Government Freebies and Cheapies* (Kensington, MD: Information USA, 1994). See also www.freebiehighway.com/government/ (accessed July 21, 2005).

15. Jane Landis, "Scholarship Search: How to Apply," *Young Money*, May/June 2005, 28.

16. Penelope Green, "Barons before Bedtime," *New York Times*, January 5, 2007, F1.

17. "Desperate Teens Sell Themselves on EBay," Associated Press, St. Joseph, MO, August 10, 2005, sfgate.com/cgi-bin/article.cgi?f=/n/a/2005/08/10/national/a064414D05.DTL (accessed January 2, 2007).

18. "Yes, I Do Windows! Community Barter Network Enjoys Success," *Baby Boomers News*, n.d., www.babyboomers.com/news/1008d.htm, 1 (accessed August 16, 2005).

19. Youth Radio, "Jobs and Money," n.d., www.youthradio.org/jobs/economics.shtml (accessed August 16, 2005).

5 Use It or Lose It: Practicalities

Allowance, paycheck, gifts, and other windfalls—enough or not enough—the total is your income, for better or worse. So what's the best way to manage it? The way you've handled money so far probably depends on the influence of your family and your own tendencies. Are you a spendthrift, a penny pincher, or somewhere between the two extremes? If you're a spender, don't worry about it too much at this point, but try to recognize the possibility that living for the moment may catch up with you later on.

As a teenager your money dealings usually come down to paying for necessities, saving a little, investing, giving to charity, and hoping and planning for enough left over to make your life, at the moment, good. Let's consider two aspects of dealing with your income: the concrete part—the physical handling of cash, checks, and other assets that come to you—and the figuring-out part; that is, estimating your expenses so that you come out even, or ahead.

HANDLING CASH

Bobby, age 20, of Sag Harbor, New York, says, "Your first thought when you get a paycheck, even if it's not much, is 'I'm going to cash it.' People my age want easy access to cash. I try to stretch out one week's pay for two weeks' expenses and then deposit every other check in my account."

"I get $60 cash weekly for lunch and dinners," says Jeff, age 15, of Merrick, New York. "The dinner money is because I go

SPENDER OR SAVER?

1. When you get money, do you usually spend it fast?
2. Do you often feel as if you don't know where your money went?
3. Do you owe anybody money?
4. Do you often misplace money?
5. Do you buy a lot of presents for family and friends?
6. Do you get a kick out of seeing money accumulate in a bank or at home?
7. Do you avoid buying things when you have to use your own money?
8. Are you willing to wait for something you want?
9. Do you often say no to something tempting?
10. Do you worry about not having enough money?

If your answers are mostly yes for 1–5 and mostly no for 6–10, you're more inclined to be a spender than a saver.

directly from school to play rehearsals a couple of times a week. I probably won't get a job while I'm still in school because of my involvement in theater, but I made $590 from tips at my summer camp job and $130 recently working sound for a show. When I get money gifts I spend half and put half in the bank. I keep my cash in an index-card box, divided up depending on what it's for."

What to do with cash is generally a fairly simple matter. Most kids keep it in a wallet, a box, or envelopes in a bureau drawer. Using a locked box may sound paranoid, but if you keep enough cash at home, consider protecting it. Now an adult, Greg, of Tenafly, New Jersey, remembers a disturbing incident in his teen years, when his summer's earnings, in cash, were taken from an unlocked box in his bedroom. Local police were able to lift fingerprints and locate the so-called friend who took the money. The "friend," charged and taken to court for this and other robberies, was found guilty and was forced to pay everyone back. What's the moral of the story? (Watch those "friends.") How about this: Avoid keeping a pile of money in your house. Use a bank.

HANDLING CHECKS

Before we talk about which bank and what type of account, here's some advice from *Wall Street Journal Classroom Edition*. If you don't have a bank account and you're thinking of cashing a check on the street at a check-cashing service, be aware that "check-cashing services can be the most expensive way to get your cash. Depending on your state's laws, the services can charge up to 5% of your paycheck—or $10 on a $200 payroll check—or even more to cash a personal check. . . . The easiest way to cash a personal check is to go to the bank named on the check. Most banks will cash checks written on their accounts, though some may charge for the service."[1]

Bank accounts are necessary for most people, so it's good to get early experience. Eighty-four percent of young customers at Bank of America open their first checking accounts before they go to college.[2]

SAVINGS AND CHECKING ACCOUNTS

The two main types of bank accounts are savings and checking. Savings accounts are for money you plan to keep for a while. You put it there and the bank rewards you by paying you interest for letting it use your money, and this interest will gradually make your savings grow. A checking account, on the other hand, is a convenience. It's a safe place to keep your

Check-cashing services charge fees at a higher rate than banks.

money until you want to pay for something by writing a check.

When you open a checking account these days, you usually receive an ATM (automatic teller machine) card. This card, when swiped in a machine, allows you to deposit money into or take money out of your account at many locations. You've probably seen ATM signs attached to banks and also in supermarkets, shopping centers, and other busy places. Some checking accounts are set up to cover an overdraft. That is, if you write a check for more than you have in the account, the bank will cover it but will charge you a high rate of interest. The trick is to avoid overdrafts. Keep track of your balance (the total you have in the account) and only write a check if you're sure you have that amount.

Notice that an ATM card may have a Visa or MasterCard logo (company symbol) on it to make it widely accepted, but

Automatic Teller Machines (ATMs) are familiar sights.

that symbol doesn't mean it's a credit card. When you hand over your ATM card to pay for something at the cash register, a clerk will often ask, "Debit or credit?" See chapter 12, "Getting the Credit," for more information on debit cards.

Before You Open an Account

Banks are in constant competition to get you as a customer. When you're in the process of choosing a bank, look for

HOW DOES AN ATM WORK?[3]

Insert your card, punch in your PIN, select which account to deposit into or withdraw from, and enter the amount of cash you want. *Then what happens?*

1. The ATM is connected by a modem to a host computer that reads the magnetic stripe on your card. It makes sure your PIN and the info on the card match.
2. The host computer is connected to your bank, which electronically gives the okay.
3. If you're depositing, the machine takes your money. (It's counted later by a bank employee.)
4. If you're withdrawing, the host computer sends an "electronic funds transfer" message to your bank to take the money out of your account and put it into the host's account.
5. The host approves your transaction and your requested money comes out.
6. Before bills come out on a tiny conveyor belt, the machine counts them and keeps track of them by means of an electric eye.
7. The details of the transaction are recorded in an electronic journal embedded in the ATM's processor. This journal can be printed out in case of any future dispute.

answers to these questions in bank ads or ask a bank representative:

1. Is there a minimum amount I need to deposit?
2. What rate of interest do I get on savings and how is the interest figured?
3. What kinds of fees and penalties will I have to pay for a checking account? How much is the ATM fee if I go for cash to another bank?
4. Is "free checking" really free, or do I have to keep a minimum balance?
5. Will I be penalized if I take out my money before a certain time?
6. Is there a nearby branch and are the hours convenient?
7. Can I do my business online?
8. Will I be welcome as a young depositor?
9. Can I get extra services, including credit cards, CDs (certificates of deposit), and loans?
10. Is the bank federally insured? Is its reputation good?

"MAY I BE EXCUSED TO GO TO THE ATM?"[4]

You need some cash at school. You have an ATM card, but it's a couple of blocks, or miles, to the nearest machine and you're pressed for time. Not a problem for kids from rural Oregon City High School or Grossmont High in El Cajon, California. Both schools have set up on-site machines for the convenience of students. In each case kids pay an extra $1.25 fee per transaction, money that goes to the school. In Oregon City the accounting class manages the machine, so in addition to being a convenience, it's a learning experience.

Security in a Checkless Society

In the future you'll probably be doing more banking *on*line than standing *in* a line at the bank. You and your friends may turn out to be the first checkless generation. A 2003–2004 banking study showed that, for the first time, more purchases were made with credit and debit cards than with cash and checks.[5]

If you do business online and/or use an ATM card, you'll need to protect your identity so that no one can pretend to be you and take money from your account. Your bank will assign you, or ask you to choose, a personal identification number (PIN), which gives you access to your account. Keep that number and your password private. Good advice is that "if you must write the PIN or password down, keep it in a safe place at home, not in your wallet. If you lose your debit card or your password and someone rips you off, you are responsible for up to $50 of losses—but only if you report the lost card or password to your bank within two days of discovering it." Delay in reporting may result in your being responsible for up to $500 of fraudulent charges.[6]

More Security Precautions

Remember that banks and computers aren't perfect. Even if you don't get a monthly statement in the mail, you're responsible for making sure that all the deposits and withdrawals in your account are accurate. Keep receipts and look online at least once a month to make sure that everything shown in your account is correct. Some debit-card purchases may not show up right away in your online account, and account balances that you get online or at ATMs may not be up-to-date. Keep personal track of what you've spent so that you don't go over your limit.

If you pay a bill online, be alert to the possibility that the transfer of funds may take some time. It's smart to pay 7 to 10 days before a bill is due to make sure your payment isn't late.

Watch out for phishing scams, that is, realistic-looking e-mails that ask you for personal information such as PINs and passwords. Your bank should never ask you for those through e-mail or unsolicited phone calls. If you're in doubt about whether you're speaking to an authorized person, hang up and call the bank back. P.S. The bank may call you if it spots anything fishy in your account, so make sure the bank has an up-to-date address and phone number.

Finally, avoid doing your bank business on a school or library computer where your dealings might not be completely private.

AN ALTERNATIVE TO BANKS

One more consideration before you decide where to bank. Have you heard of credit unions? If not, you're among the half of eligible people who are "not very familiar" or "not at all familiar" with credit unions and the services they offer.[7] Credit unions are nonprofit financial institutions owned by their members and organized for their benefit. Members usually have something in common, such as working for the same employer or belonging to the same union or church. If your parents or other relatives belong to a credit union, they can arrange for your membership.

Credit unions, which offer personal attention, are alternatives to banks.

Most credit unions offer almost the same services as commercial banks, but their fees and loan rates are lower. How come? "Credit unions are . . . true cooperatives, owned by members," says Bill Hempel, chief economist of the Credit Union National Association. "They exist to please members, not stockholders, as banks do."[8]

Another good point about credit unions is that because they're usually small operations where employees recognize and maybe even know you, you're likely to be treated as one of the family—a far cry from banking at a big branch office or online. On the other hand, a possible negative is that "while many credit unions belong to ATM networks, those networks tend to be far less extensive than a bank's, meaning you could face some of those ATM fees."[9]

CHOOSING YOUR BANK

Okay, you've gotten advice from relatives and friends, you've read brochures, and you've compared rates and other information online. Now you're ready to choose your bank. By the way, until you reach the age at which your state no longer views you as a minor, any account of yours will have to be custodial—that means an adult must open it for you, in his or her name and yours. For that reason it may be easiest to bank where your family banks. That institution may actually waive a fee as a way of welcoming you.

If you intend to do your banking mainly by mail or online and you consider kid-friendliness important, you may want to think about the Young Americans Bank in Denver, Colorado. Founded in 1987, this is the first and only state-chartered, FDIC (Federal Deposit Insurance Corporation)-insured bank exclusively for young people under the age of 22, with nearly 15,000 customers across the United States.[10] It claims its customers are treated with respect, receive easy-to-understand booklets, and are offered many services, such as checking, ATM cards, savings accounts, credit cards, CDs, travelers' checks, and personal loans.

But if you want to be able to do what your parents and grandparents have done for decades—walk into a bank or credit union, inhale the odor of the place, and receive cash in your hands from a real person (a teller)—then you may want to choose a local bank. Warning: Some bank names sound cooler than others. Try not to make a decision based solely on the name.

BUDGETING

Let's talk now about planning how to use your money, otherwise known as budgeting. According to money writer Tere Drenth, "Establishing a budget is the act of deciding how much of your money you're going to spend on one item, how much on another, and so on—before you're actually in the position of spending the money. . . . Sticking to a budget—which is not the same as establishing a budget—is the act of following through on those decisions. Creating a budget isn't easy, but sticking to any budget is extremely difficult."[11]

Most people find budgets annoying. You write down your income, or what you hope will be your income. You list expenses, but a lot of them are guesses and sure to be inaccurate. You try to stay within your limits, and then the price of something shoots up, or you give in to some temptation, and your budget is a bust. If you mistrust budgets enough, you may be able to wing it without one. Nathan Dungan, in *Prodigal Sons and Material Girls*, says, "I know people who use budgets and those who don't. The ones who do say it helps keep things in balance. Those who don't admit to feeling anxious about their 'throw caution to the wind' approach." He suggests talking to friends who do and friends who don't keep a budget in order to decide which ones you feel are doing best.[12]

Money writer Jayne A. Pearl says, "I have never used a formal budget. As a freelance writer, my income is unpredictable. . . . Yet I usually manage to make ends meet without writing lists of expenses and income. . . . So why do I recommend teaching kids how to budget? . . . Because kids do have fairly predictable and uncomplicated sources of income (allowance and jobs) and expenses."[13]

It figures that getting into the habit of budgeting while you're young and flexible should make it easier to budget when you're an adult and the stakes are higher. Apparently lots of Americans never practiced budgeting, because "the average American family carries almost $9,000 in credit card debt."[14]

If you're wondering whether you need a budget, ask yourself whether you have even one unmet financial goal. "No goal is too big or too small, as long as it's important to you. . . . If you're having trouble reaching your goal, you need a budget."[15]

The best reason to have a budget is to achieve the feeling that you're in control of your finances.

How to Set Up a Budget

Let's say you're convinced. How do you start making a budget? With a pen and notebook, probably, but computer software programs are also popular. Some examples are

Quicken, Microsoft Money, Managing Your Money, and Mvelopes Personal. If you go the pen-and-notebook route, it makes sense to start with recording expected income (allowance, jobs, gifts, borrowed money); then list typical outlay (what you spend your money on), starting with necessities, or things you can't eliminate.

Some money experts suggest you launch your budget by setting aside a certain amount for savings first to make sure that money doesn't get lost in the shuffle. For instance, we're told in *Business and Personal Finance* that Tyrone "considers his savings as a fixed expense. He writes himself a check for $75 before he pays his bills; then he sends his check for immediate deposit into his savings account."[16] Other people like to vary savings, depending on what is left over at the end of each month.

What to Include in Your Budget

1. Repayment of debts
2. Lunch, snacks, and other food
3. Clothing
4. School supplies, fees, club dues, and other school stuff
5. Personal supplies and services
6. Gifts for friends and family
7. Savings
8. Charitable contributions
9. Entertainment (movies, events, trips, CDs, computer games, etc.)
10. Books, magazines, hobbies, miscellaneous

Keeping Track of Expenses

Estimating your expenses, based on past weeks or months, is obviously only the beginning. The challenge of budgeting is to save receipts and jot down the price of everything you buy so you can keep track of whether your guesses were on target or not. Mel Stiller, of Consumer Credit Counseling Service of

Southern New England, suggests, "Carry around a notebook for a month and write down everything you spend. No purchase should be too small to record. At the end of the month annualize your costs—that is, multiply how much you spent by 12 to estimate how much you might spend in a year."[17]

An advantage to paying expenses by check and/or using a debit card is that your checkbook record and debit card statement are already your receipts. It's not a bad idea to divide notebook pages into three columns: one for the expenditure, one for estimated cost, and one for actual cost. Then, at the end of the week or month, you'll total up your columns, compare estimates with actual costs, and see if your budget was realistic. If you haven't been realistic, you'll have to take a look at what expenses can be trimmed. Or else you'll have to figure out how to add to your income. Keep your budget flexible. The main points of it are to avoid wastefulness, to help you reach financial goals, and to give you peace of mind.

If at First You Don't Succeed

If your budget doesn't work out at first, don't be too annoyed with yourself. In future attempts, see if any of these suggestions help. If you have to borrow from one category— let's say, savings or charity—to pay for transportation or food, make a special effort as soon as you can to replace the amount you borrowed from yourself. If you find that savings are always getting ignored, try doing what Tyrone does—deducting savings first, putting them out of reach in the bank. If you think you've failed partly because your written budget is too complicated, try to simplify it. Or if the way you're recording— in a notebook or with computer software—isn't working, try a different method. Good luck.

NOTES

1. Karen Blumenthal, "Got Money?" *Wall Street Journal Classroom Edition*, September 2004, 18.

2. Blumenthal, "Got Money?" 18.

3. Eve Drobot, *Money, Money, Money: Where It Comes From, How to Save It, Spend It, and Make It* (Toronto: Maple Tree Press, 2004), 54–55.

4. Laura Randall, "This Is Convenience Banking: A.T.M.'s in Schools," Education Life, *New York Times*, November 7, 2004.

5. Karen Blumenthal, "Warning: The Future Is Here," *Wall Street Journal Classroom Edition*, September 2005, www.wsjclassroomedition.com/archive/05sep/cons_edsep.htm, 1 (accessed October 8, 2005).

6. Blumenthal, "Warning," 1–2.

7. Jacob Dirr, "Are Credit Unions Right for Me?" *Young Money*, January/February 2006, 9.

8. *Home & Family Finance: Personal Finance Information from Your Credit Union*, Madison, WI, 2005.

9. Blumenthal, "Got Money?" 18.

10. Key Corp, "Young Americans Bank First in Colorado to Sign ATM Agreement with KeyCorp," Press Release, June 12, 2003, www.snl.com/Interactive/IR/file.asp?IID=100334&FID=1212705&OSID=9 (accessed October 8, 2005).

11. Tere Drenth, *The Everything Budgeting Book* (Avon, MA: Adams Media Corp., 2003), 2.

12. Nathan Dungan, *Prodigal Sons and Material Girls* (New York: John E. Wiley, 2003), 158.

13. Jayne A. Pearl, *Kids and Money* (Princeton, NJ: Bloomberg Press, 1999), 80.

14. "Teens Spend Money, Want Credit, Need Education," *NCL Bulletin* 64, no. 2 (March/April 2002), nclnet.org/finances/teens.htm (accessed October 11, 2005).

15. Drenth, *Everything Budgeting*, 4.

16. Jack R. Kapoor, Les R. Dlabay, Robert J. Hughes, and William B. Hoyt, *Business and Personal Finance* (Woodland Hills, CA: Glencoe/McGraw Hill, 2005), 83.

17. Karen Blumenthal, "Making Ends Meet," *Wall Street Journal Classroom Edition,* March 2005, 16.

6 Laughing All the Way to the Bank: Saving

Having some money saved makes most people happy. If you're not a natural saver you may be surprised that "saving money is important to American teens; about nine out of ten save money, though 36 percent admit that they're saving for specific items they want to purchase. Almost one-quarter (22 percent) are saving for college and 27 percent for no particular reason. Four out of ten say they save half or more of their money, and three out of four have a savings account."[1]

BENEFITS OF SAVING

Why save? The answers are pretty obvious, but just in case you need to be reminded, "we save for three reasons," says money writer Neale Godfrey. "First, for protection in case of an emergency; second, for retirement; and third, to buy something we really want."[2] Retirement may not be on your mind yet, but you have to admit that the other two reasons make sense. And why save in a real bank instead of stashing money in a drawer? As we've said before—to keep your money safe and to increase it by earning interest.

The earlier you start saving, the better off you'll be when you're older. Arthur Berg Bochner, who cowrote with his mom *Totally Awesome Money Book for Kids and Their Parents*, began investing at age 10, and by the time he was 14, he was worth $100,000.[3]

Bochner is an actual person, but here's the story of a hypothetical person named Jessica. If Jessica, after college,

WHAT IS INTEREST?

Interest works like this: You and a lot of other people put money in a bank, money you intend to leave there for a while. The bank lends this money, for a set amount of time, to other people. When that time is up, borrowers have to pay back the borrowed amount (the principal) plus a usage fee. This usage fee, a certain percentage of the principal, is called interest. The bank keeps some of this interest and they pay some of it to you and other depositors.

There are two kinds of interest: simple and compound. Simple interest on $1,000 at the rate of 3 percent per year, for instance, would earn you a simple $30 at the end of one year. Compound interest is better because the bank pays interest on your interest. For instance, if you deposited that same $1,000 in an account with 3 percent interest compounded monthly, after five years you would end up with $1,161.62. If you're interested in determining compound interest, type "Compound Interest Calculator" into an Internet search engine and follow the instructions. P.S. When you're shopping for a bank, look for one that compounds interest quarterly, monthly, weekly, or even daily. Computing interest can be a complicated thing—that's why people hire accountants.

saves and invests $2,000 a year from her salary for nine years (at 10 percent interest) and adds no more money to that investment of $18,000, she'll have $839,396 by the time she's 65.[4] Unfortunately 10 percent interest is unusual these days.

Before we get involved in how and where to save, let's clarify what we mean by *savings*. First there are short-term savings, money you set aside so you can, in a fairly short time, pay for something like a computer, a vacation, or even a car. This money is only savings temporarily. It's really deferred spending.

Second, let's divide long-term savings in the following way: money earmarked for big, possibly once-in-a-lifetime expenses, such as a college education, a wedding, a condo, or a house; money set aside to be left untouched for emergencies, such as job loss or illness; and money you can spare at the moment—you're not sure what you'll eventually spend it on—to be invested in order to make the principal grow.

Even if you're not interested in being a serious investor, all your savings may as well be earning interest—as opposed to weighing down your piggy bank or making a bump in your mattress. And there's no need to worry about the safety of your savings if you deposit them in a bank insured by the Federal Deposit Insurance Corporation (FDIC). The FDIC insures your savings up to $100,000.

HOW TO BEGIN

You might get into the habit by choosing a goal that's exciting. Is there anything you really want that seems out of reach? Even if it takes a material reward to get you to save, saving may start to feel natural. A suggestion from *Young Money* magazine is "to start small and allow your saving habit to grow along with your money. Commit to saving all of your loose change for 30 days. As you break a dollar put the change aside," and at the end of the month take the coins you've accumulated and open a savings account. Let that be a start to committing larger amounts.[5]

Or maybe you can find a partner, and an incentive, in your parents or grandparents. Ask them what they think of contributing matching funds to your savings account. That is, for every dollar you put in, they add one. You can tell them about these parents, for instance:

"Cindy Swikard, who co-owns with her husband a landscape construction company and a travel agency in San Diego, opened a savings account, with an initial deposit of $500, for each of her six kids (ages 12 to 17) when each turned 10. 'Any money they put in the account from the time they were 10 until they turned 16 we would match. . . . This money is theirs; they have access to it. But if they take money out of this account, they must replace it before we start matching again."[6]

Another example comes from David Owen, who says, "I decided to open a bank of my own. I called it the First National Bank of Dad, and I invited my children to become my first (and only) depositors. . . . I said I would pay them interest on their balances at the rate of 5 percent per month. . . . Compounded monthly, that works out to an annual rate of more than 70 percent." According to Owen, this arrangement, plus other incentives, sent his kids diving under the sofa cushions for lost change and turned them into savers.[7]

TYPES OF SAVINGS ACCOUNTS

So far we've been talking mainly about putting money into savings accounts in commercial banks, credit unions, or savings and loan (thrift) associations. When you open a savings account, you'll keep track of your deposits and withdrawals in one of two ways. Either you'll receive a passbook, a little booklet in which you write down your transactions, or else you'll receive a statement in the mail from your bank at the end of each month or so.

After you've been depositing for a while, you may want to consider switching your savings to another type of account, where you'll get a higher rate of interest. Here are three safe possibilities, all easily available wherever you do your banking:

1. **Money market accounts. These are savings accounts (you may write a limited number of checks) in which the interest rate varies. You pay a small fee, trained people make safe investments, and you earn a little more interest than if your money was in a straight savings account.**

2. **Certificates of deposit (CDs). These are savings alternatives in which you deposit money (usually a minimum of $500) for a set time period (from one month to five or more years). The rate of interest goes up slightly the longer you leave your money in, and there's a penalty for taking your money out before the CD comes due.**

3. **Savings bonds. These are issued by local, state, and federal governments; by nonprofit organizations; and by corporations. You're lending them your money, and they promise to pay you back in a stated amount of time at an agreed-upon rate of interest.**

All three of these saving options will give you a little higher rate of interest than a regular savings account, and all three are safe. Money market accounts have the advantage of allowing you to write checks. CDs are worth buying if you don't mind tying up your money for a stretch. And U.S. savings bonds are thought to be particularly safe because they're issued by and guaranteed by the federal government. (The most popular is the

Buying government Series EE Bonds is a safe long-term way to save.

Series EE Bond.) Rules and rates differ on all of these investments, so it's important to shop around and make comparisons.

IRAS

If you have a solid job, one more super-responsible way of saving money is to start an IRA, or Individual Retirement Account. You may remember a reference to IRAs at the end of "Landing a Job" (chapter 3). In order to be eligible for an IRA, you have to be earning money that you're paying taxes on. So if you're making money but aren't reporting your income to the government, you can't get into an IRA. If you're paying taxes, then in 2007 you're allowed to contribute up to $4,000 to an IRA. Starting in 2008, you may contribute $5,000 a year.

The point of an IRA is that you're not only saving money and earning interest but you're also deferring some of your taxes. Instead of paying now, you'll pay later, probably at the stage when you're retired and are in a lower income bracket. Unfortunately, if you take money out of an IRA early you pay a 10 percent penalty, so it's best to think in terms of keeping your money in the IRA until you're 59 1/2 .

There are several variations on the way IRAs are set up. In the case of one called a Roth IRA, your money is taxed up front and then accumulates, including interest, to be taken out, five or more years later, tax free. According to *The Motley Fool Investment Guide*, "The younger you are, the more you should tend to open a Roth. Paying taxes now in order to rack up decades worth of compounded returns, eventually withdrawing *all* of it . . . that's a sweetheart deal."[8]

A Rollover IRA lets you transfer some or all of your contributions to another plan if you change employers. Educational IRAs, also known as Coverdell Education Savings Accounts, allow "individuals to contribute up to $2,000 per year toward the education of any child under 18. The contributions are not tax-deductible. However, they do provide tax-free distributions for educational expenses."[9] A Simplified Employee Pension Plan (SEP-IRA) is an arrangement in which both you and your employer contribute. The SEP and the Keogh are specially designed plans for self-employed people and their employees. In short, if you're already earning a decent income, get further information and advice about IRAs from your boss or any person who has had direct experience.

STILL RELUCTANT TO START SAVING?

If you need further encouragement to put away money now that you won't see for years, here are some "for instances" that may help you get the point.

If a 15-year-old invests $1,000 a year for five years in any kind of IRA and then makes no more contributions, at age 65 (assuming a 9 percent annual growth rate) the account would be worth $289,225.[10]

Let's say that Sue has a part-time job for her last two years in high school and in that time contributes to an IRA a total of

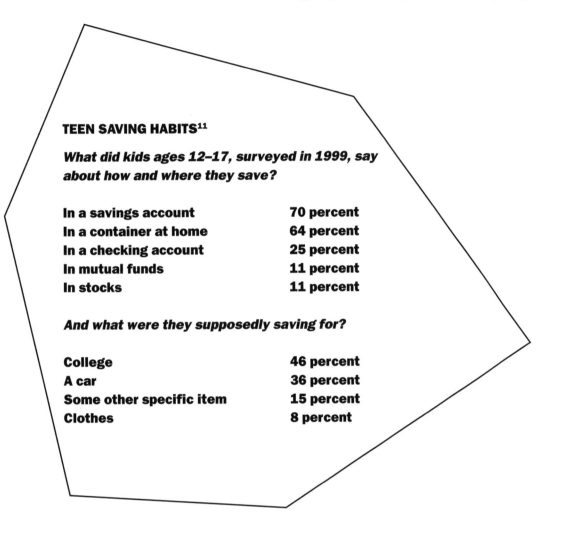

TEEN SAVING HABITS[11]

What did kids ages 12–17, surveyed in 1999, say about how and where they save?

In a savings account	**70 percent**
In a container at home	**64 percent**
In a checking account	**25 percent**
In mutual funds	**11 percent**
In stocks	**11 percent**

And what were they supposedly saving for?

College	**46 percent**
A car	**36 percent**
Some other specific item	**15 percent**
Clothes	**8 percent**

$3,000. If she continues to work part-time and contribute in college, she would accumulate almost $465,000 to be accessed at age 60.[12]

Meanwhile, college sophomore Amanda puts $1,000 in an IRA each year until retirement and ends up with $582,000. With a traditional IRA she'll have to pay $145,000 in taxes when she takes the money out, but if she contributes $1,000 in post-tax dollars to a Roth, she can keep the whole $582,000.[13]

The message here is that interest *compounded*, whether in an IRA or any other account, makes your money grow and grow. Remember that an IRA must be custodial. That is, depending on where you live, you're considered a minor until age 18 or 21, and as a minor you'll need the help of an adult to open the account.

INCENTIVES FOR THOSE WITH LOW INCOME

Saving is impossible if you're poor, right? Not necessarily. New programs these days are being devised to help people save through IDAs, or Individual Development Accounts. These programs use public or private funds to set up savings accounts for people of low income. "There are now more than 500 such projects across the country, whose participants have opened more than 20,000 accounts. . . . They must save at least $10 a week and attend a series of financial-planning classes. IDA savings must be used for college, job training, buying a home, or starting a business."[14]

The wave of the future will probably be for the government to encourage every young American to get involved in long-term saving. Legislation has been introduced in Congress, through the ASPIRE (America Saving for Personal Investment, Retirement, and Education) Act, to provide a Kids Investment and Development Account to every American child born after December 31, 2006. If the ASPIRE Act becomes law, every baby born in the United States starting in 2007 who receives a Social Security number will automatically have an account opened for him or her, with a one-time $500 contribution from the federal government. Children from households earning less than the national median income will be eligible for another $500. This plan, already in effect in 81 other countries, is intended to encourage savings, promote financial literacy, and expand opportunities for young adults.

Kids and their families will be urged to make voluntary contributions along the way, and eligible kids will be given matching funds. Each account, which will grow to be about $20,000, may be redeemed starting at age 18, to be spent only on education, home ownership, or retirement. At any point after age 18 the account holder will be allowed to roll over unused funds into a Roth IRA, already described.[15] Although you were born too late to profit from the ASPIRE Act, your children and grandchildren may be beneficiaries in years to come.

Even if you can manage to put aside only a little at this point in your life, do as much as you can and laugh all the way to the bank.

NOTES

1. "Teens Spend Money, Want Credit, Need Education," Teens and Finances Column, *NCL Bulletin* 64, no. 2 (March/April 2002), nclnet.org/finances/teens.htm, 1 (accessed October 11, 2005).

2. Neale S. Godfrey, *Money Doesn't Grow on Trees* (New York: Simon & Schuster, 1994), 23.

3. Jayne A. Pearl, *Kids and Money* (Princeton, NJ: Bloomberg Press, 1999), 53.

4. Susan Shelly, *The Complete Idiot's Guide to Money for Teens* (Indianapolis, IN: Alpha Books, 2001), 85.

5. Sanyika Calloway Boyce, "Answers to Top Student Money Questions," *Young Money*, March/April 2006, 32.

6. Pearl, *Kids and Money*, 46–47.

7. David Owen, *The First National Bank of Dad* (New York: Simon and Schuster, 2003), 20.

8. David and Tom Gardner, *The Motley Fool Investment Guide for Teens* (New York: Fireside, 2001), 257.

9. Jack R. Kapoor, Les R. Dlabay, Robert J. Hughes, and William B. Hoyt, *Business and Personal Finance* (Woodland Hills, CA: Glencoe/McGraw Hill, 2005), 493.

10. Citizens Funds, "Custodial IRA," n.d., www.citizensfunds .com/individual/tools/retirementplanningcenter-custodialira.asp (accessed October 18, 2005).

11. "Exposure to Financial Education on the Rise, Merrill Lynch Teen Survey Finds," April 9, 2005, www.icrsurvey.com/Study .aspx?f=ML_Teens.html (accessed January 2, 2007).

12. "IRAs for Teens," n.d., www.unionfederalbank.com/ learning-center/financial-library/retirement/iras-for-teen, 2 (accessed November 9, 2005).

13. Gardner, *Motley Fool Investment Guide for Teens*, 137–38.

14. Jackie Calmes, "Saving Grace," *Wall Street Journal Classroom Edition*, March 2006, 13.

15. "Background Information on KIDS Accounts and the ASPIRE Act," n.d., www.results.org/website/article.asp?id=838 (accessed January 2, 2007).

7 How Does Your Money Grow? Investing

You've heard of the stock market, right? And investing and Wall Street? Wall Street is an actual street in the financial district of New

"I initially thought that investing was something rich people did to get more money. Now I understand that the majority of people can invest. I began investing in order to buy a nice used car."—Tristan, age 15[1]

York City where investors transact business in their offices and at the New York Stock Exchange. But Wall Street is also a term used to refer to all buying and selling of stock. After you've gotten experience earning interest from checking, savings, and money market accounts and from bonds, CDs (certificates of deposit), and IRAs (Individual Retirement Accounts), you may want to go for higher stakes by investing in the stock market. And even if you don't have the financial means now, it won't hurt to know how the market works, in case you're in a different position later on.

Maybe, like humorist Rick Horowitz, you're amazed at hearing about people your age who invest. "They're all over the place," he says. "Thousands and thousands of kids whose idea of a good time is checking out their coolest stocks' latest moves. They join high school stock clubs. They play stock-market games on the Internet. And they spend real money on real stocks in the real world. Why aren't these kids hanging out on street corners the way they're supposed to?"[2]

Wall Street in Lower Manhattan, New York City, is the prime center of stock and bond trading in the United States.

WHAT DOES IT MEAN TO BUY STOCK?

With a little extra money and the patience to inform yourself, you, too, can check out cool stocks. Let's say you have a friend who's been making a profit selling T-shirts. She would like to expand her business but needs more cash in order to advertise and to buy supplies. So you chip in. You aren't a full-fledged partner; you're only buying a piece of her business. The two of you make an agreement that she'll pay you back, on a regular schedule, a certain percentage of her capital (what her business is worth). You hope, of course, that she'll do fantastically, so you'll get back much more than you put in.

Chances are, if you actually invest, it won't be as direct as an arrangement with a friend. More likely you'll buy stock from a big company and have no personal connection with the people

New York Stock Exchange.

who run it. But the principle is the same. A stock represents a single share of ownership in a company, and when you own a stock, you're actually a part owner of a corporation. You will probably buy your stocks through a broker, a trained advisor who works for a brokerage house (investment company). He or she will make the purchase on your behalf . This process of buying or selling the stock is called writing a ticket. When brokers write a ticket for you, they get a commission and so does the brokerage firm.

WHY TAKE RISKS?

If money market bank accounts, CDs, and government bonds are safe and buying shares of stock is riskier, why take a chance on the stock market? Because if you're careful and smart you can end up with more. Is that greedy? Not from the standpoint of *The Motley Fool Investment Guide for Teens*, which urges you to strive for financial freedom so that you'll be able to fulfill your dreams, enjoy life more, avoid stress, help others, and make your mark on the world. "Some people avoid the stock market because *it's too darned risky*," says the Motley

Fool. "Believe it or not, over your lifetime as an investor, it's riskier *not* to invest in the stock market. . . . If all your savings is in a bank account earning three percent per year, on average, then your money will gain no ground on inflation. A dismal circumstance."[3] P.S. Depending on the economy, interest on savings may be even lower than 3 percent.

So what do we mean by *risk*? The possibility that you'll lose some or all of the money you've invested. Every investment carries some risk, even a savings account. But by taking some risk you may greatly increase your chance of earnings, and an investment in stock isn't anything like the level of risk involved in gambling. Note: you have a better than 99.9 percent chance of *losing* the money you spend on a lottery ticket.[4]

"The best risk-reduction tool is knowledge," David Gerlach says in *Young Money*. "Never invest in something you don't understand. Always consider how an investment fits into your long-term goals. Always try to calculate, at least roughly, both the best that is likely to happen with a given investment and the worst. . . . Even a very good investment performance takes few people into the Rolls Royce showroom. On the other hand, even relatively bad performance should not force you into auctioning your furniture on eBay. Risk can't be eliminated, but it can be understood, respected and managed."[5]

What's the Worst That Can Happen?

Some older Americans are still affected by the worst-case scenario of risk. They either lived through or felt the effects of the stock market crash in October of 1929. At that time, after a 10-year boom sent stock prices very high, the bubble burst and stocks plummeted in value. What followed was the Great Depression, a long period during which thousands of investors lost everything. Banks, stores, and factories closed, so that millions of people were jobless, homeless, and penniless. It took time, World War II, and certain changes—such as the creation of the Federal Deposit Insurance Corporation (FDIC) and new investing rules—for the economy of the United States and the rest of the world to recover from the Great Depression.

A less severe, but still serious, downturn in the stock market occurred in October 1987, when the Dow Jones average lost more than 500 points in one day. In spite of such risks, though, the Motley Fool says, "We think that the best place for your long-term money is in the stock market" because "over the long run, the overall stock market has gone up. And up. And up and up and up. In fact, the stock markets of the United States over the past hundred years have been among the great wealth creators in the history of the human species."[6]

How about Bonds?

Investing in bonds may put you at less risk than investing in the stock market. But some bonds are chancier than others. "The risk ranks like this, from lowest risk to highest: government bonds—that is, savings bonds and treasuries [see chapter 6]; then municipal bonds—that is, bonds of cities, counties and states; and then corporate bonds—that is, bonds of private companies like Kellogg or Pepsi. Still, even when you invest in corporate bonds, you do not have the risk levels that you have with stocks."[7]

GETTING STARTED IN THE MARKET

Let's say, though, that you're going to live dangerously and invest in the stock market. When do you begin? When you're young, all the experts say, so that your money has the maximum time to grow. Here's some general advice:

- Wait until you're out of debt and have some money you can afford to lose.
- Don't invest money in stocks that you're going to need in five years or sooner.
- Inform yourself by reading, exploring sites on the Internet, taking a course, or joining an investment club.
- Get help from someone knowledgeable, such as a parent or teacher.

Whether you want it or not, for legal reasons you'll need the collaboration of an adult if you're under 18.

A possible starting place is buying shares in a mutual fund, which means you and thousands of other investors jointly own a bunch of different stocks in many companies. A professional does the buying and selling, and you and the other investors are paid out dividends, which you can take out in cash or reinvest in the fund. Buying mutual funds lowers your risk, because even if some companies in the fund do badly, others may do very well. Another advantage is that many mutual fund companies are kid friendly, meaning that they let you open an account with a minimum amount of $250 or $500.[8]

Because there are more than 7,000 mutual funds of various types—such as growth, growth and income, international and global, bond funds, index, tax-free, sector, load and no load— it's obvious that you'll want specific information and good advice before investing in them. Disadvantages of mutual funds are that service fees to the fund will be deducted from your assets and paying taxes on your earnings can be complicated. One kind of mutual fund is of particular interest to beginning investors—index funds, which usually charge very low fees. The Motley Fool says that index funds "demand no research and outperform the majority of funds on the market."[9] Also check out *exchange-traded funds* (ETFs) on the Internet or in an investment guide.

GETTING IN TRAINING TO CHOOSE YOUR OWN STOCKS

Okay, mutual funds aren't enough challenge. You want to pick your own stocks. As we keep saying, there's a lot to learn, and one way to go is to join an investment club. First look close to home. Maybe your school offers investing as a course or an extracurricular activity. If not, a lot of information is a few clicks away on a computer. For instance, the website Consumer Reports for Kids encourages kids to form investment clubs as casually as they may have once started fan clubs. And on www.fool.com/Investment Club/Investment Club.htm, you can make contacts with others who want to share investing expertise and responsibilities.

Depending on where you live, you may find colleges or banks and other business organizations that offer seminars or competitions for people your age. The University of Cincinnati's Economics Center, for instance, sponsors a Stock Market Game, which thousands of kids play at school twice a year. The players invest a mock $100,000 for 10 weeks. Among kids who played the game in middle school were some who, when they got to high school, formed the Mariemont Green Envy Club, sponsored by the local Kiwanis. Green Envy members pay $10 each into the club fund each month. After studying stocks, visiting companies, and discussing possibilities, they make decisions as a group about what stocks to buy.[10]

Stock market simulations (investment games that use imaginary money) are easily found on the Internet. The principle behind these games is that you have a hypothetical amount of money—maybe $100,000 or $500,000—to invest. Over a period of one to three months you "buy" and "sell" stocks on the basis of your research and your hunches, and you see, at the end of the period, whether you've made a fantasy profit or suffered a fantasy loss.

Wall Street Sports is an example of a stock market simulation in which you trade professional athletes instead of securities and win prizes such as T-shirts and trading cards. School classes and/or investment clubs often compete in these games as a group. Some simulations offer real prizes, including shares of stock. A well-known competition of this kind is the Stock Market Game, sponsored by the Securities Industry Foundation for Economic Education. The popularity of this game has increased enormously over the last decade, and it is played now by students in 15 or more countries.

Another way to learn about investing is in summer programs like the four-week LEAD program conducted at the University of Pennsylvania's Wharton School and at 10 other business schools around the country. LEAD introduces several hundred high-achieving high school kids per year—especially minority students—to economics, finance, marketing, and investment banking. Along with taking courses and visiting corporations and NASDAQ (National Association of Securities Dealers Automated Quotation) headquarters in New York, the participants work in teams to create fictional businesses. One student had a choice between a trip to Italy and Wharton's LEAD program. "I chose LEAD and I thought I was going to regret it," says Amanda Jimenez of Newark, New Jersey. But at the end of four weeks she decided to study marketing in college, joining the 65 percent of LEAD graduates who go into business.[11]

It's possible, of course, acting on your own, to get a foot in the door of the stock market without joining a club or taking a course. According to James Cramer, when he was a kid his family "had two board games—one was called *Stocks and Bonds* and the other was called *Acquire*—and I played them until I wore them out. I also developed my own stock market game in fifth grade, which I showed to my class. . . . Just like you want your team to win, I wanted my stocks to win," says Cramer, who grew up to be president of Cramer, Berkowitz & Co. and a daily financial columnist.[12]

"I was thirteen when I bought my first stock," says Jonathan Steinberg, chief executive officer of Individual Investment Group. "I took $1,000 of my bar mitzvah money and invested in Abbott Laboratories. I made about a 30 percent return. . . . From the age of thirteen I was reading the *Wall Street Journal* every day plus several business magazines."[13]

TEACHING YOURSELF ABOUT THE MARKET

Even if you don't begin trading stocks in the cradle, picking your own stocks can be challenging and fun. How do you decide which one or ones to buy? The Motley Fool suggests that rather than relying on advice from others, ask yourself what fascinates you most. Computers? Then focus on learning about companies like IBM, Dell, Gateway, Sun Microsystems, or Microsoft. You love video games? Explore Sony and Activision. Clothes? Check out Abercrombie & Fitch, the Gap, or American Eagle Outfitters. Media and entertainment? Learn about Viacom, General Electric, and Walt Disney. You like food? Think about buying stock in McDonald's, Starbucks, or Whole Foods. List your interests, where you shop and eat, and what products and services you yourself use, and then make a point of finding out what the ticker symbols are for the companies you like.

A ticker symbol is "an abbreviation for a company's name that is used as shorthand by stock-quote reporting services and brokerages. For example, Kellogg's ticker is K, Coca-Cola's is KO, and the Dynamic Materials ticker is BOOM." You'll need to know the ticker symbol to track the performance of the companies you're interested in, in the stock listings of a newspaper or on the Internet. Of course making good stock purchases involves more than just following your personal interests.[14] For more information about the economic

Ticker symbols seen in lights at the New York Stock Exchange.

history of companies and how to make decisions about what to buy, consult *The Motley Fool Investing Guide for Teens*, *The Young Investor*, and other sources credited at the end of this chapter.

When you're at the point of being ready to make a stock purchase, you'll need to select a brokerage firm and open an account. A broker in the firm will facilitate your buying and selling of stocks and will charge you a customer fee for the services that he or she performs. Some well-known brokerages include Charles Schwab, Fidelity Investments, E*TRADE, TD Waterhouse, Merrill Lynch, Salomon Smith Barney, and Morgan Stanley Dean Witter.

Just as there are guidelines for choosing a bank, there are considerations in choosing a brokerage firm. Maybe you'll go

STOCK MARKET TERMS

▶ *bear market:* a trend in the overall market to lose value (perhaps 10 percent or more) over a period of time.

▶ *bond:* agreement between two parties allowing one to borrow from the other for a set amount of time in exchange for interest

▶ *broker:* licensed person who buys or sells stocks and bonds for individual investors

▶ *bull market:* market that has been gaining value over a period of time

▶ *capital:* money or other assets used to start and run a company

▶ *commission:* fee paid by investor to broker for making a transaction

▶ *common stock:* type of stock that provides the most basic kind of corporate ownership and entitles owner to voting privileges

▶ *dividend:* payout, usually four times a year, from a company to its shareholders

▶ *Dow Jones Industrial Average, or "the Dow":* a scorecard that shows how the New York Stock Exchange did that day; this measurement is based on the closing price, in the form of an average of 30 actively traded major American companies

▶ *New York Stock Exchange (NYSE):* one of the major U.S. exchanges where stocks are traded; two others are AMEX (the American Stock Exchange) and NASDAQ (the National Association of Securities Dealers Automated Quotation)

▶ *portfolio:* stocks and bonds in a mutual fund, or stocks and bonds owned by an investor

▶ *preferred stock:* type of stock that gives owner the advantage of receiving cash dividends before common stockholders receive any

▶ *shareholder:* person who owns stock in a company

▶ *stock:* shares of ownership in a company

with the broker of your parents or an experienced friend. Or maybe you'll look in the Yellow Pages for a brokerage that's close to where you live. Chances are you'll go to the Internet, where most brokerages have websites, and you'll look for answers to some of these questions.

1. Is the brokerage one that is strictly online, or are there convenient local branches so that you can deal with a real person once in a while?

2. If you're interested in mutual funds, does the brokerage offer the funds you're interested in?

3. Is there a minimum amount you need to open an account?

4. **What are the commission rates? That is, how much will it cost you to buy and sell stocks? Try to spend no more than 2 or 3 percent in commission, which means sifting through a lot of information to make sure of that rate.**

At the Motley Fool's Discount Brokerage Center, you can learn a lot more about how to evaluate brokerages and how to deal with them.[15]

Opening an account involves filling out an application, which you mail in or hand-deliver, along with a check or cash. As we've already said, if you're a minor you need a parent or guardian to go with you. The brokerage will give or send you an account number and maybe a password. Depending on the brokerage and the type of account, you may also get an ATM card and checks to write on the account.[16]

Once you own stocks, of course, you'll need to keep track of how they're doing. If they're doing well, you'll probably hang on to them, and if they aren't, you'll have to decide whether to wait out a bad patch or to sell. Tristran Robinson, a 20-year-old University of Pittsburgh student, believes in buying and holding, that is, purchasing an undervalued stock and holding on to it for a while to give it time to increase in value. Tristran did this with his first buy, Synovus, and watched it grow more than 10 percent over the past five years.[17] Decisions to buy and sell are tough to make, even for experienced investors, and even experts are often wrong. If, like Tristran and thousands of other young people, you become fascinated by the stock market and hooked on the game-like aspects of it, you'll probably enjoy doing the research that's necessary to be a successful investor.

Don't forget that if you make enough profit on investments you'll have to pay taxes on them. Specifically, "if you are under 14, you are allowed to earn $1,400 a year on your investments without paying taxes to the U.S. government. If your savings and investment accounts earn more than $1,400 a year, the excess will be taxed at your parents' income tax rate."[18]

Let's hope you do so well in your investing experiments that you won't even feel the burden when you have to pay taxes.

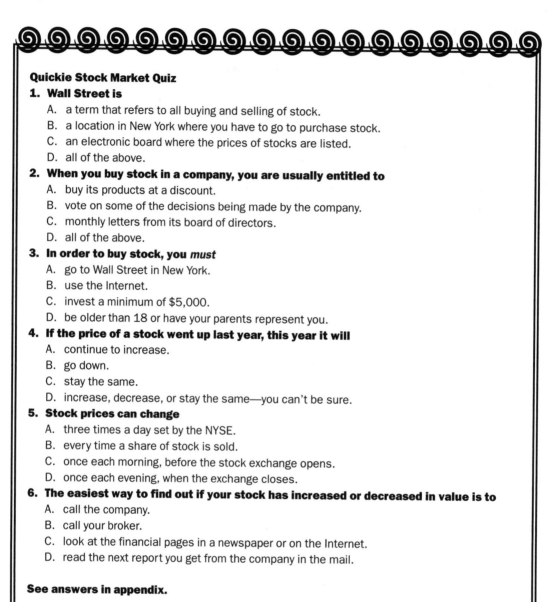

Quickie Stock Market Quiz

1. Wall Street is
   A. a term that refers to all buying and selling of stock.
   B. a location in New York where you have to go to purchase stock.
   C. an electronic board where the prices of stocks are listed.
   D. all of the above.

2. When you buy stock in a company, you are usually entitled to
   A. buy its products at a discount.
   B. vote on some of the decisions being made by the company.
   C. monthly letters from its board of directors.
   D. all of the above.

3. In order to buy stock, you *must*
   A. go to Wall Street in New York.
   B. use the Internet.
   C. invest a minimum of $5,000.
   D. be older than 18 or have your parents represent you.

4. If the price of a stock went up last year, this year it will
   A. continue to increase.
   B. go down.
   C. stay the same.
   D. increase, decrease, or stay the same—you can't be sure.

5. Stock prices can change
   A. three times a day set by the NYSE.
   B. every time a share of stock is sold.
   C. once each morning, before the stock exchange opens.
   D. once each evening, when the exchange closes.

6. The easiest way to find out if your stock has increased or decreased in value is to
   A. call the company.
   B. call your broker.
   C. look at the financial pages in a newspaper or on the Internet.
   D. read the next report you get from the company in the mail.

See answers in appendix.

NOTES

1. Selena Maranjian, "True Teen Stories," The Motley Fool, www.fool.com/teens/teens09.htm, 3 (accessed November 9, 2005).

2. Rick Horowitz, "Young and in Love—with Money," March 30, 1999, yesrick.com/033099.htm, 1 (accessed November 20, 2005).

3. David and Tom Gardner, *The Motley Fool Investment Guide for Teens* (New York: Fireside, 2002), 100; original emphasis.

4. Gardner, *Motley Fool Investment Guide*, 101.

5. Douglas Gerlach, "Understanding Risk & Volatility," *Young Money*, March/April 2005, 22.

6. Gardner, *Motley Fool Investment Guide*, 101.

7. Bateman, *Young Investor*, 32.

8. Janet Bamford, *Street Wise: A Guide for Teen Investors* (Princeton, NJ: Bloomberg Press, 2000), 114–15.

9. Gardner, *Motley Fool Investment Guide*, 57.

10. Annie-Laurie Blair, "Teens Carefully Take Stock," *The Enquirer*, February 5, 2005, http://news.enquirer.com/apps/pbcs.dll/article?AID=/20050205/BIZ01/502050346/1076/ (accessed November 21, 2005).

11. Susan Snyder, "Business Schools Attempt to Lure Bright Minorities into Their Sectors," *Philadelphia Inquirer*, Knight Ridder Tribune Business News, August 2, 2003.

12. Bamford, *Street Wise*, 95.

13. Bamford, *Street Wise*, 105.

14. Gardner, *Motley Fool Investment Guide*, 169–73.

15. Selena Maranjian, "Start Investing," The Motley Fool, n.d., www.fool.com/teens/teens05.htm, 4–5 (accessed October 18, 2005).

16. Maranjian, "Start Investing," 3.

17. Tina Dressel, "Glad He Started Early," *Young Money*, November/December 2005, 22.

18. Bateman, *Young Investor*, 106.

8 Better to Give: Supporting Charities

Chances are you yourself are struggling to stay afloat financially. Maybe you're feeling you should be on the receiving end of charity instead of handing it out. So why be generous when that kid in gym class asks for a contribution for a homeless shelter? You don't have to give. You can duck out on school collections; toss away letters of request from your place of worship; and ignore pleas, on TV and live, to help victims of a flood. But if you actually have a heart and don't want to be labeled a Scrooge, admit that giving usually makes you feel good.

WHY BE GENEROUS?

Money writer Susan Shelly says, "Personally I think that social responsibility is understanding your place in the world, doing what you can to help sustain others, and respecting and protecting the environment. . . . Being socially responsible doesn't mean you need to join a group of monks and sleep on a hard bed. . . . It simply means being aware of and appreciating what we have and helping others when we can."[1]

Consider why most people give and why you may want to, too. A 2005 Harris survey showed that as many as 15 million youth nationwide donated $926 million to victims of the December 2004 Indian Ocean tsunami, and another 5 million kids collected relief money from others for the same relief effort.[2] In this case, as in the case of the U.S. hurricane Katrina disaster in Louisiana and Mississippi, almost everyone was aroused by mass suffering. Besides the obvious reason for helping others—because it's the right thing to do—here are a few other considerations when you're asked to open your wallet.

- You might be in the same boat someday, hoping that others will help you.
- If society as a whole is well off, usually we profit as individuals. On the other hand, if a society is poor, not much will be collected in taxes, and what tax money there is will be spent to alleviate poverty.
- The U.S. government, to encourage giving, lets taxpayers take a deduction for most charitable contributions. Many people like the idea of giving money to a favorite charity and at the same time reducing the amount they pay in taxes.

This tax benefit is one reason why billionaires establish organizations to give away money. Another reason is that some wealthy people, like Bill Gates, are committed to giving help to those who need it most. William Henry Gates III, founder of Microsoft and one of the richest Americans, started the Bill and Melinda Gates Foundation, which has given grants for health and education totaling over $7 billion since its inception in 2000.[3] Based on the idea that successful philanthropists can do much more good work if they have much more money, Warren Buffett, in June 2006, arranged for approximately $37 billion of his fortune to go to the Gates Foundation. Even if you never find yourself in a position to establish a foundation, you may get satisfaction from donating whatever you can afford.

GIVING TIME AND GOODS INSTEAD OF MONEY

Of course it's possible to be charitable without ever giving away a penny by donating used items to those who need them or by offering your time. Many organizations collect clothes and household items to aid victims of disasters, and many groups, such as schools, hospitals, and soup kitchens, welcome teenage volunteers. Walking, running, or bicycling for a cause—that is, collecting money from sponsors—is another popular way to be generous without depleting your own bank account.

An alternative to giving money to a charity is giving your time.

ARE ALL CHARITIES EQUAL?

Assuming you're a giver, how do you decide which causes to give to? Do you carry cash around in order to be ready to donate at any moment? These questions lead to the bigger one—what is your attitude and how do you act when someone asks for a contribution? The range of answers from people your age looks something like this:

- "I give money if I can because I budget it that way. Sometimes I tell the person to come and ask me tomorrow."—Shanieka, age 17

- "Getting asked for money is pretty awkward and annoying, because the person asking never knows if you're in a bad situation. But if I can, I will give."—Kandace, age 18

◎ **"I don't usually give because I never know if it is for a real cause."—Donna, age 17**

◎ **"I have no job, so I kindly say no."—Rachel, age 17**

◎ **"Giving to charities is something I will do when I have more money."—Jahmel, 18**

In some schools charities are well regulated by teachers or other supervisors, so you can be pretty sure your contribution won't end up in a classmate's pocket. If no responsible person seems to be sponsoring the collection, or if you've never heard of the charity, or if you don't approve of the cause, or if you don't personally know the one who's asking for money, you may decide, like Rachel, to kindly say no—or, like Shanieka, to postpone giving until you get more information. Advice from the teenage guide *Dollars and Sense* is, "If someone asks for a donation to an organization you've never heard about, take your time to make a decision. Do not respond immediately and do not ever give cash to a stranger at your door."[4]

ASKING FOR CONTRIBUTIONS

How do you feel about being on the asking end—approaching friends or strangers with the hope that they'll make contributions to your charity? Some people feel comfortable—even noble— soliciting money for a cause. But what if the "charity" is the prom or the football team? Such fund-raising often involves the sale of candy or other merchandise. There's often pressure to sell and to buy in these situations. Some kids engage in this kind of exchange happily. "I don't really ask for contributions when I'm fund-raising with candy in school," says Denise, age 17. "People usually just come up to me." Others find it awkward to ask for money or to push overpriced items to kids who may be strapped. What do you think? Are school fund-raisers harmless, useful, and fun, or do you think the school budget should include all expenses of extracurricular activities?

It's pretty hard to ignore the pitch of a friend who corners you directly for a contribution, but you have time to consider requests on TV or ones that come in the mail. These are usually aimed at your parents, but even if you aren't on any charity mailing lists yet, you will be, and sooner or later you'll have to face questions like, who is most deserving? And how do you decide how much to give? Maybe your family already has a plan for settling these questions. If you and your family are members of a religious group, you may already be contributing on a regular basis. But if you haven't been involved in family decisions regarding charities up to this point, you might offer your two cents—especially when it comes to donations to nonreligious (nonsectarian) organizations.

METHODS OF GIVING

Families such as the Feders of Montclair, New Jersey, use the following arrangement. For the last seven years or so at holiday time, *New York Times* writer Barnaby J. Feder and his wife, Michele, have gathered their three children, 11, 13, and 15 years old, for a family evening of charitable giving. After reading through solicitations that have come in the mail in the preceding months, each child gets to donate $100 to charities of his or her choice. As a way of assuring that the kids are choosing wisely, Feder and his wife have them write a short letter to each selected charity, explaining why they've chosen those organizations.[5]

Shel Horowitz, author of *The Penny-Pinching Hedonist*, uses a similar system. After chucking out solicitations from groups he disagrees with, he puts the rest in a file, and every six months he; his wife, Dina Friedman; and their two kids open the file and decide jointly which organizations to support.[6]

A broader-scale example of cooperative giving is found at the Gideon Hausner Jewish Day School in Palo Alto, California, where seventh graders take an actual course in learning how to do "the work of the world." Kids in the class choose philanthropies, research them, make presentations, narrow down their choices, and pool their contributions. Instead of giving each other gifts for their bar and bat mitzvah ceremonies, they contribute a comparable amount of money to the common fund.[7]

Let's say, though, that you're going to give on your own, apart from your family. Of all the organizations that make pleas on radio and TV, through the Internet, and by mail, how do you decide which ones are worthiest? You may get special satisfaction by giving to those closest to home, that is, to local food banks, shelters, or scholarship funds. Or, if a family member or friend has suffered a particular illness or other bad break, you may want to contribute to the national organization that gives aid and sponsors research in that area.

EVALUATING CHARITIES

How do you avoid being taken—giving your money to groups that pay inflated salaries to their administrators, or worse, giving it to crooks who set up charity scams? According to Asa Aarons, TV consumer reporter and columnist, "Hurricane Katrina, like all natural disasters, is bringing out the best and the worst of human nature. Although many Americans are eager to help the victims, others may try to profit from post-catastrophe generosity."[8]

TIPS ON CHARITABLE GIVING[9]

- ▶ For a contribution of more than a dollar or two, pay by check instead of cash—a check made out to the charity, not to the person collecting.
- ▶ Don't be fooled by names of organizations that look impressive or that closely resemble names of well-known groups.
- ▶ Remember that you aren't under obligation to send money to groups that send you unordered merchandise, such as greeting cards, stamps, or pens. These organizations tend to have high fund-raising costs.
- ▶ If you're considering giving money to solicitors on the phone, door-to-door, or on the street, ask enough questions to assure the charity is legitimate. For starters, ask for the group's full name and address and for the collector's ID.
- ▶ When you're asked to buy candy, magazines, and the like, ask what part of the total goes to the charity, in order to figure out what you're actually giving to the cause.

Luckily there are ways to check the practices and reputations of charitable organizations at your local library, through your state attorney general's office, or most easily on the Internet. The Better Business Bureau claims that more than 80 percent of the money raised by charities in this country comes from individuals, and to help donors make wise giving decisions they have set up the Wise Giving Alliance (www.give.org). On this website, you can find out whether a charity is on the alliance's approved list, what work it specializes in, and exactly how it will be spending your money. You can also access a brochure called "Tips on Charitable Giving" (see sidebar on the previous page) that outlines how to evaluate mail appeals, what to do about unwanted mail, and when tax-exempt doesn't mean tax-deductible. Another online source of information on charities is Guidestar (www.guidestar.org).

NOTES

1. Susan Shelly, *The Complete Idiot's Guide to Money for Teens* (Indianapolis, IN: Alpha Books, 2001), 36.
2. "New Survey Indicates as Many as 15 Million Youth Nationwide Have Donated Up to $926 Million to Tsunami Relief," February 9, 2005, www.harrisinteractive.com/news/printerfriend/index.asp?NewsID=890 (accessed January 2, 2007).
3. Bill & Melinda Gates Foundation, "About Us," n.d., www.gatesfoundation.org/AboutUs/ (accessed September 20, 2005).
4. Ernestine Giesecke, *Dollars and Sense: Managing Your Money* (Chicago: Heinemann Library, 2003), 28.
5. Barney J. Feder, "A Family That Pays Together," *New York Times*, November 15, 2004, F1.
6. Jayne A. Pearl, *Kids and Money* (Princeton, NJ: Bloomberg Press, 1999), 121.
7. Karen Alexander, "Turning a Traditional Time to Get into a Lesson in Giving," *New York Times*, November 15, 2004, F6.
8. Asa Aarons, "Eager to Be Charitable? Think before You Give Aid," *New York Daily News*, September 19, 2005, 38.
9. BBB Wise Giving Alliance, "Tips on Charitable Giving," www.give.org/tips/giving.asp (accessed August 16, 2005).

g You've Got the Power! Teen Spending

Are you aware of how important you are to the marketers of this country—that is, to all the shopkeepers, retail salespersons, and people selling stuff on the Internet? If you're ever worried about being popular, console

> "I am definitely not a cautious spender. When I know of a particular product I want, I go out and get it without regard to the price."—Yaw, age 17
>
> "I always look for the sales. Rarely do I buy anything at full price."—Jamal, age 17
>
> "When I am not with a parent I am a very cautious spender. When I'm with a parent I'm still careful, just not as careful."—Arielle, age 17

yourself with this: *I'm loved by people who sell things.* No matter how poor you, personally, may think you are, your teenage generation is the wealthiest in American history.

TEEN SPENDING

Of course there are a lot of you—more than 30 million. Kids your age hit a spending peak in 2001, and now, after a couple

ARE YOU A MARKETER'S DREAM?

1. Do you spend more than half of your income?
2. Do you often eat meals outside your house?
3. Do you choose your own clothing?
4. Does your family consult you before buying food, computers, and home entertainment equipment?
5. Do you own a car or motorcycle?
6. Do you have your own telephone line, DSL line, or cell phone?
7. Do you go out at least twice a week to movies, sports events, and such?
8. Do you have at least one major hobby or pastime that costs money?
9. Do you give gifts on a regular basis to family and friends?
10. Do you use personal services such as hair and nail salons, gyms, or spas?

Five to 10 yes answers make you a marketer's dream.

of years of a strained economy, are coming back with an average increase in spending of 5 percent a year. In 2004, as a group, you managed to spend $169 billion, and that doesn't include the $278 billion your parents and guardians spent on you. In the United States, "total teenager spending exceeds the gross domestic product of countries such as Finland, Norway, Portugal, Denmark and Greece."[1]

These big numbers are overwhelming and a little silly, so let's talk about you as an individual. Figures from 2004 show that teens aged 12 to 19 spent an average of $91 per week. This amount includes your total income—allowance, other money from parents, what you earn, and gifts.[2] You may be looking in your wallet and thinking, "Spending power? Some other kids, maybe. Not me." But the truth is, no matter how little you spend, you're still important to marketers, who are as interested in little profits that add up as they are in big killings. They're also hoping that your buying power will increase in the future and that, even if they have to wait, they'll hook you someday.

Spending for What?

So what is all this teenage money going for? According to a 2003 study by Coinstar, "Teens spend 33 percent of their weekly earnings and allowance on clothing and an additional 21 percent on food." As you might guess, other major expenses include movies, music, and games.[3] These entertainment expenses, by the way, may sound like a sad joke to teens whose families are among the 37 million in the United States who are classified as living in poverty.

But most Americans spend, and, aside from loving you for your own personal outlay, marketers like the influence you have on your family. When it comes to computers and iPods, you may know more than your parents, so it's no surprise that you're considered the experts who are targeted by sellers.

How should you use all this power? Even if you're thinking, "I don't have power," almost everybody buys something. Whatever you spend your money on, and whether it's a lot or a little, these obvious guidelines make sense: if you need to be careful with money, avoid buying stuff you don't need or suspect you may soon get tired of; look for the best quality at the lowest price; and try to stay within your budget, whether it's a formal written budget or a rough idea in your head.

P.S. If you're lucky enough not to have to worry about every penny, skip advice that doesn't apply. Almost everybody would like to buy a favorite item instead of the cheapest, or buy two things instead of one. And who wouldn't prefer to shop in a place that's convenient and attractive, with great service? Sometimes it's worth it, or absolutely necessary, to go to the closest store, even if you can't really afford to. But assuming you want to be as careful with money as possible, where should you shop?

Where to Shop

By now you may already have a routine. Are you used to going to stores close to your home or ones your family has been patronizing for years? Depending on where you live, you may have access to malls or be limited to a few small stores. These days, of course, you can also shop on the Internet.

As you surely know, online shopping is growing in popularity with teenagers. After a slow start, merchants have figured out that you operate differently than adults. As a result, companies like Macy's, Alloy, bolt.com, and gurl.com are offering you websites that Nathan Dungan refers to as "virtual malls."[4] "Teens are so demanding of 'what's in it for me' that unless the site offers everything they want, they'll reject it," says Jane Buckingham, president of a consulting company in New York. A study by Teenage Research Unlimited shows that boys have slightly more experience buying online than girls, and more than half of 16- and 17-year-olds have shopped online.[5] That percentage will undoubtedly increase in the years to come.

Saving on Necessities

Probably a lot of your purchases are things you absolutely can't do without, such as food outside your home, certain items of clothing, and personal or school supplies. Later we'll discuss purchases you *want* more than you *need*. Meanwhile, is it possible to save on those things you can't eliminate?

1. *Food.* Take food and drinks from home or buy stuff in a supermarket as an alternative to eating in restaurants, or get take-out food and share the expense with friends. Drink water in restaurants instead of beverages that cost money. Choose restaurants with fixed-price meals or ones that accept coupons. Think twice about going to restaurants where the price will escalate because of the tip.

2. *Clothes.* Buy clothing out of season and at other sales. In season, ask if a sale is coming up. Try brands without fancy labels. Avoid buying clothes that require dry cleaning. Consider thrift shops (or occasional borrowing from a sibling or friend).

3. *Supplies and services.* Buy store brands that are the equivalent of more expensive products. Purchase in large quantity, at a discount store, things you use all the time. Look for "loss leaders" at discount stores—products sold below cost as bait to lure you in. Exchange services with willing and able friends or relatives instead of paying money to tutors or hair and nail salons.

If you're a person who doesn't mind second-time-around items—if you like the challenge of stretching your money— think about heading for the nearest Salvation Army, like 15-year-old Gaby Yosca of New York City. Gaby recently bought "four dresses, an aqua-tinted tank top, a brown corduroy blazer, two silk shirts, two belts, a pocketbook, and a book about makeup for a grand total of $62.50." She's one of a new breed of dollar-conscious teenagers, kids who either need to be careful with money or who spend cautiously as a matter of principle. As Irma Zandl, a youth marketing consultant, says, "It's cool to be smart about how little you spend."[6]

Buying to Feel Good

Let's say you're being as careful as possible in buying necessities. You're saving a certain percentage of your income

If you don't mind second-time-around items . . .

and giving some to charity. What about your discretionary income? (The amount you have left to spend after necessities have been covered.) Spending your discretionary income is, or at least ought to be, fun. If your favorite pastime is shopping, you already know what scientists are proving in labs—that shopping makes you feel good, at least for a little while.

"Much of the joy of shopping can be traced to the brain chemical dopamine. . . . Dopamine is associated with feelings of pleasure and satisfaction, and it's released when we experience something new, exciting or challenging. And for many people, shopping is all those things," according to Tara Parker Pope in *Wall Street Journal Classroom Edition.* "MRI studies of brain activity suggest that surges in dopamine levels are linked much more with anticipation of an experience rather than the actual experience—which may explain why people get so much

pleasure out of window-shopping or hunting for bargains."
Pope says that if you're aware that shopping triggers off a
chemical change in your brain, you may be more careful
making decisions. You might, for instance, walk away from a
possible purchase and come back for it the next day only if
you're sure you still want it.[7]

WHEN THE JOY TURNS DARK—SHOPLIFTING

Speaking of clear-headed decisions, sometimes teenagers slip
up. We can't discuss shopping without a mention of "one of
our nation's darkest secrets," shoplifting. There are about 23
million shoplifters in this country, 25 percent of them kids.
Shoplifting not only hurts the offender and the store, but it
also overburdens the police, results in lost tax dollars for
communities, and causes the innocent majority to have to pay
more for goods. Shoplifting is said to be an addiction, treatable
but hard to conquer. Are you among the 86 percent of kids
who say they know other kids who shoplift? Help is available
for offenders from groups such as the Honest to Goodness
Project and the National Association for Shoplifting
Prevention.[8]

ARE COMMERCIAL MESSAGES STEERING
YOU RIGHT OR WRONG?

You can't be living in this society without knowing that you're
the target of advertisers. If you're an average kid, you see
about 40,000 television commercials a year. As a group teens
spend almost 40 hours a week with radio, TV, movies,
magazines, and the Internet. Children of parents with low
incomes watch more TV than those whose parents have
higher incomes. The average kid lives in a home with three
television sets, two CD players, three radios, a video game
console, and a computer. Two-thirds of kids between 8 and 18
have a TV in their rooms.[9] Unless your family is one of the
few that limits television viewing to an hour a day of the

> **STORY OF A SHOPLIFTER**[10]
> "When I was 12-years-old, I was what you might call a kleptomaniac. . . . My family had some serious financial problems. . . . It was like we'd hit rock bottom. . . . The people I hung out with never seemed short of cash. . . . So-called friends introduced me to the dead-end world of stealing. Sometimes I felt a speck of guilt, but not near enough to make me stop. . . .
>
> "One day I was in the mall with a new friend of mine. We decided to go steal some tapes and CDs. We each had one and were walking out of the store when out of nowhere the guard came up to us. . . . He escorted us to the back of the store, told us to sit down and played back the tape where they recorded us stealing. . . . After that they took pictures of us with a Polaroid camera, and made files with our names on them. They placed handcuffs on our wrists and escorted us downstairs. . . . When we got to the police station, they told us to call our parents. When asked what happens if we decide not to call them, he said that we would have to go to the detention center until Monday.
>
> "When my mother came she was angry. . . . But I could tell that more than anything else she was hurt. I was assigned a probation officer. . . . I was caught two more times. . . . When I was 15, I was sent to live in a group home. . . . Over time I began to change at the group home. I started talking to a therapist, getting out some of my anger. . . . I started writing stories and now I've got a part-time job and when I want money, I earn it."

Discovery Channel, chances are you're being bombarded by TV ads.

Now that it's possible to skip TV commercials by using devices attached to your set, such as TiVo, advertisers are becoming more aggressive. They're finding new ways to get their messages to you. Some companies are sending text messages directly to individual cell phones. Some are sending e-mails, including ones that invite you to participate in games or contests. Others are using gimmicks such as CD-ROMs inserted in magazines.[11] If you want to shut out commercial messages, you have to be very determined. Most teens and adults allow themselves to be swamped.

Effects of Commercial Messages

What's the big deal about seeing and hearing so many commercials? They're not going to kill you, are they? Probably not, if you're aware of advertisers' methods and you evaluate their messages sensibly. But it's good to be skeptical of magical promises and especially on your guard with certain products that may affect your health. For instance, considering that you're seeing over 30,000 commercials a year for fast food, candy, cereal, and toys, is it possible that you're craving and buying more sweet and fattening stuff than is good for you? Studies show that every hour of TV watched per day results in a greater chance of obesity.[12] Food marketing executives admit that they're trying to convince you that their products will make you popular. Think about conserving your money and health by gaining popularity in some other way.

Some marketers want to hook you now so that later you'll buy their products. You've seen 75,000 ads for alcohol by the time you reach driving age. "More teens cited Budweiser as their favorite commercial than any other brand in a 2002 study." According to a report in the state of Washington, the tobacco industry spends $237.8 million a year in that state on marketing.[13] These marketers are encouraging you to spend your money and to put your health at risk.

ADVERTISERS' SNEAK ATTACKS

Before we concentrate further on the question of how to be a smart consumer, let's consider the sneaky ways that marketers try to rope you in.

Social Networking

In order to figure out what your attitudes are toward fashion, entertainment, technology, health and beauty, and food, online research agencies like Look-Look recruit thousands of so-called teen trendsetters to report what "you" like.[14] Some marketers use that information to take a next step. Has an acquaintance of yours recently been raving about a certain cosmetic? Or maybe a person at school has sent you a text message recommending a new movie. These may simply be well-meaning friends, but there's another possibility: your friends are being used by advertisers.

Procter & Gamble (P&G), for instance, sellers of health and beauty products, uses a technique called social networking. This gimmick is also called viral marketing—viral as in virus, something that spreads and spreads. Social networking or viral marketing works like this: A company, such as P&G, locates "connectors"—popular teens with broad social networks and a supposed interest in "discovering and telling others about relevant new ideas." P&G leaks information about products to the connectors, who spread the word to friends. What's in it for the connectors? Sometimes actual money rewards. More often, free products, scripts of popular TV shows, and maybe a sense of importance. In 2002 the number of connectors was projected at 150,000.[15] Next time somebody you know gets carried away about a product, ask yourself, "Is this for real, or am I talking to a connector?"

A variation on this approach is "cool hunting." Market researchers call in teenage "correspondents" for conferences and ask various questions: What music do you like? What do you wear? Which of these products are cool or uncool? Researchers sell the information they get to marketers, who then try to create and promote "cool" products. Some marketers, such as Sprite, sponsor events like hip-hop concerts, often with a tie-in to the media. Kids are paid to attend the concert, where the company's logo is displayed and MTV cameras are rolling. A mere five companies control most of what teens are likely to spend money on: music, films, TV, books, CDs, clothing, amusements, and sports teams. The big five are the Rupert Murdoch empire, Disney, Viacom, Vivendi SA, and AOL-Time Warner. If you don't like monopolies, try making your purchases from other marketers, but you may have trouble finding them.[16]

Brand Names in Sit-Coms

Okay, you're tired of being targeted. You're relaxing in front of your TV, and commercials are over—temporarily. But what's that? A Ford truck on a cop show? Ragu spaghetti sauce on a weekly sit-com? A brand-name computer game on a reality show? "On television, once upon a time, there were shows, and there were commercials. And you could tell the difference. The screen went black for a second between them. But with audiences for network television shrinking, and more viewers zapping through commercials on recorded TV, the standard 30-second ad is no longer a very reliable way to reach viewers. So some of the industry's most powerful advertisers are increasingly securing roles for their products inside prime-time sitcoms and dramas."[17]

In other words, marketers hire agencies to place their products in TV shows in such a way that you'll easily recognize brand names. Without prior knowledge of this, you may think the product placement is accidental instead of what it really is—a sneak attack by advertisers.

Product placement has also been introduced into feature films. Because movies are so expensive to make, many filmmakers are happy to weave real products into their scripts in exchange for the illusion of realism and for money to help finance the film. These arrangements often result in cooperative deals, such as a Baskin-Robbins store, in collaboration with the movie *Shrek 2*, promoting a flavor of ice cream called Shrek's Swirl.

Is there anything wrong with this idea of embedding products in entertainment shows? Watchdog groups warn that blurring the line between content and advertising is unfair to viewers. If and when certain products such as prescription drugs appear in a TV show there could be complications for the advertiser and the viewer. It makes sense to be alert to hidden messages whenever you're a viewer of TV or movies.

Ads at School

But at least you're free of ads during those long hours at school, right? *Wrong.* Not if you're among the 7 million students in more than 11,000 schools who see a 12-minute current events program each day on Channel One. If you're in that number, you're actually seeing only 10 minutes of news—plus 2 minutes of commercials. In the years since 1990, when Channel One first appeared in schools, parents and educators have argued about it.

On the one hand, the channel has won prizes for its coverage of important issues. On the other hand, its many critics accuse Channel One of presenting the news in an oversimplified way and, in its ads, making ignorance sound cool, emphasizing physical attractiveness, and encouraging bad eating habits.[18] Another complaint is that taxpayers end up spending millions to finance schools where kids are watching commercials. The teaching time lost to those commercials is equivalent to a whole school day per year.[19]

Even if your school doesn't subscribe to Channel One, chances are you're still a captive to commercial messages during the school day. Are any of your textbooks, book covers, study guides, or computer software provided by sponsors with something to sell? Companies often give teachers attractive classroom kits, but the hitch is, according to a Consumer Union review, that 80 percent of the kits examined were biased and/or inaccurate and obviously promoted the interests of the company.[20] In one case a subversive teacher, supplied with book covers featuring ads of Nintendo, Gatorade, and Secret deodorant, had the kids cover books backside out, so the ads wouldn't show.[21] What do you think? Should schools welcome company freebies or not?

It's easy to see why administrators of poorly funded schools would be tempted to make deals. And it's even easier to see why corporations would like to get a foot in the school door. Exxon Mobil, for instance, distributed videos that showed them as environmentally friendly after they got a bad rap from an Alaskan oil spill.[22] Here are some other examples of businesses intruding on your school day:

◎ **American Passage Media Corporation installed billboards in high school locker rooms, where they reached 3 million students.**

◎ **American Express funded "Academies of Travel & Tourism" at four New York City high schools.**

◎ **Burger King and Sprite placed ads on school buses—a popular but controversial new location for commercial messages.[23]**

Naming Rights

A big discussion these days is whether schools should sell naming rights—that is, allow businesses to name buildings in exchange for serious money. In a much-publicized case, the small Brooklawn, New Jersey, school district got a $100,000 donation from a local supermarket and named its new gym the ShopRite of Brooklawn Center. Other examples, since then, are Rust-Oleum Field at Vernon Hills High School, north of Chicago; the Eastern Financial Florida Credit Union stadium at Everglades High School; and a $55 million School of the Future, under construction in Philadelphia, that will be paid for mostly with private money. Do you know anybody who wants to name a science lab for $50,000, or a food court/cyber café for $500,000?[24]

Ads in Schools: Good Idea or Bad?

You may be thinking, so what? How are ads in school hurting me? Sofia, age 16, says, "It's a marketing procedure and it does no harm to anyone." Her classmate Atira, age 18, adds, "I don't really think it's wrong. Advertising is advertising—they flaunt it any chance they get." A lot of watchdogs do mind, though—experts who don't want you to be unfairly influenced or caught up even more in the desire for things, things, things. They're also concerned that situations like this might become common: "In 1998 Mike Cameron, a senior at Greenbrier High School in Evans, Georgia, was suspended for wearing a Pepsi T-shirt on the day the school was participating in Coca-Cola's 'school-sponsored Coke day,' a national competition with other schools to win $10,000."[25] Wouldn't you like to be free to wear whatever T-shirt you want?

Speaking of beverages. Are there vending machines in your school? Coke, Pepsi, and Snapple are among the companies that make deals with school systems. They'll give money—for a new gym, let's say—if the school agrees to install machines that sell only their products. Nathan Dungan says, "I give American schools two F's. One for failing to teach basic consumer finance. The other for failing to protect children from predatory marketers." Beverage contracts may sound harmless, Dungan says, but a 10-year exclusive contract between Coke and the Colorado Springs school district required that they sell at least 70,000 cases of Coke products during one of the first three years, or payments to the school would be significantly reduced.[26]

Even if you love Coke and your school is receiving much-needed money, you may want to consider these questions: Should schools be taking any money at all from businesses? Should schools favor one company over another? Should schools be encouraging kids to eat and drink snacks and beverages that aren't good for their health?

You're part of a group that collectively spends billions. Marketers are out there like sea creatures with tentacles. How can you enjoy yourself and at the same time protect yourself as a shopper? By learning to find the best buys.

NOTES

1. Ann Holdsworth, "Teens Cash In," *Fiscal Notes*, August 2005, www.cpa.state.tx.us/comptrol/fnotes/fn0508/teens.html, 1 (accessed January 12, 2006).

2. Teenage Research Unlimited, "TRU Projects Teens Will Spend $169 Billion in 2004," December 1, 2004, www.teenresearch.com/PRview.cfm?edit_id=287 (accessed January 12, 2006).

3. Holdsworth, "Teens Cash In."

4. Nathan Dungan, *Prodigal Sons and Material Girls* (New York: John Wiley and Sons, 2003), 54.

5. National Craft Association, "Online Spending Trends," www.craftassoc.com/teenagespending.html (accessed January 12, 2006).

6. Ruth Laferla, "Teenagers Shop for Art of the Deal," *New York Times*, September, 22, 2005, G5.

7. Tara Parker Pope, *Wall Street Journal Classroom Edition*, February 2006, 5.

8. National Association for Shoplifting Prevention, "Public Education and Statistics," www.shopliftingprevention.org/WhatNASPOffers/NRC.htm, 1 (accessed March 1, 2005).

9. Susan Linn, *Consuming Kids* (New York: New Press, 2004), 5.

10. Norman Brant, "Not So Easy Money," *New Youth Communications*, n.d., www.pbs.org/newshour/on2/money/shoplift.html, 1–5 (accessed September 26, 2004).

11. Suzanne Vranca, "Changing the Channel," *Wall Street Journal Classroom Edition*, March 2006, 6–7.

12. Common Sense Media, "Media Facts," www.commonsensemedia.org/resources/media_facts.php (accessed January 20, 2006).

13. Jolene Gensheimer, "Parents Can Help Teens Spot Media Hype," *Parent Map*, January 2005, www.parentmap.com/jan_05/0105_5b.htm (accessed February 28, 2005).

14. Dungan, *Prodigal Sons*, 83.

15. Dungan, *Prodigal Sons*, 71–72.

16. "The Merchants of Cool," PBS *Frontline*, FROL1909, aired 2004.

17. Brian Steinberg and Suzanne Vranca, *Wall Street Journal Classroom Edition*, December 2004, 8–9.

18. Mark Crispin Miller, "How to Be Stupid: The Lessons of Channel One," *Extra*, May/June 1997, cited on the Fairness & Accuracy in Reporting website, www.fair.org/index.php?page=1384 (accessed February 6, 2006).

19. Linn, *Consuming Kids*, 82.

20. Linn, *Consuming Kids*, 81.

21. "Ads in Schools," *Online NewsHour*, May 20, 2002, www.pbs.org/newshour/bb/education/jan-june02/ads_5-20.html (accessed February 6, 2006).

22. Ramin Farahmandpur and Peter McLaren, "Corporate Sponsorship Threatens Quality of Education," *Advertising Educational Foundation*, January 2, 2007, www.aef.com/industry/news/data/2000/1262 (accessed January 2, 2007).

23. Farahmandpur and McLaren, "Corporate Sponsorship."

24. Tamar Lewin, "In Public Schools, the Name Game as a Donor Lure," *New York Times*, January 26, 2006, www.nytimes.com/2006/01/26/education/26schools.html?ex=1295931600&en=e2e6822851c816f6&ei=5090&partner=rssuserland&emc=rss (accessed February 8, 2006).

25. Farahmandpur and McLaren, "Corporate Sponsorship."

26. Dungan, *Prodigal Sons*, 93–96.

10 Time to Say Good Buy: Getting Your Money's Worth

You're the one who has to decide if you're going to be a smart buyer. Parents, guardians, friends, and advice books can nudge you, but getting the best value is basically up to you.

"When a commercial comes out for a new video game with crazy graphics, it makes me want to go out and buy it. I pay attention to TV commercials the most, because I watch TV a lot."—Jamal, age 17

"I shop at designer places. I'm used to dressing up with a croc or a moose. I'd never shop in ***."
—Keith, age 16

"I look online at different styles and compare prices. If the store with the good price is too far away, I go to the next best place."—Kofi, age 16

"It's more expensive to be out of school than in school because you're always looking for something to occupy your time."—Will, age 18

WHERE TO SHOP?

Places	Advantages
1. Major department stores	Everything under one roof, wide selection, recognizable brands, ease of returning merchandise, comfortable surroundings
2. Small, privately owned shops	More personal attention (usually), specialized merchandise
3. Discount stores	Low prices, wide selection (sometimes), recognizable brands (usually)
4. Outlets	Low prices, often on name brands
5. Catalogs	Convenience
6. The Internet	Competitive prices, convenience
7. Street vendors, flea markets	Low prices
8. Thrift shops and yard sales	Still lower prices

IF YOU'D LIKE TO SPEND LESS, ASK YOURSELF . . .

- Do I buy mainly because I enjoy shopping, regardless of whether I have an actual need?
- Am I hooked on certain designer labels? And if so, can I afford the extra expense or not?
- Is it possible I'm being snowed by commercials? Would I be better off tuning them out?
- Am I overpaying because I'm lazy, because I don't take time to find good buys? Or is my time worth more than the extra money I sometimes pay?

SOME CONSUMER TIPS

If you're satisfied with yourself the way you are, fine. But let's assume you'd like to be a smarter consumer. Here's some advice from *The Everything Budgeting Book*.[1]

- If buying a quality item will wreck your budget, save up and wait or make do with a less expensive version.

◎ Don't assume that higher prices always mean higher quality. Sometimes prices are inflated to make you think you're getting the best.

◎ When you buy items such as electronics, look them up in the monthly magazine *Consumer Reports*. This organization's tests are reliable and unbiased. They don't accept advertising so they don't owe anyone. *Consumer Reports* is available in most schools and libraries, and its website is also helpful.

◎ Don't pay extra for quality if you're not planning to keep an item very long. A lifetime guarantee isn't always necessary.

BRAND NAMES COST MORE

Another word about designer brand names. You may be tired by now of adults clucking over teenagers' supposed need to follow the crowd. Most of us care about what our friends—and even strangers—think of us. Almost nobody wants to be seen as unattractive. But if you're getting into financial trouble by overspending in an attempt to be popular, wouldn't it be smart to *get over it*? Do you really want to be loved for your collection of designer jeans?

Also, what if you pay for labels and people don't even recognize your outfit as the real thing? There are lots of good, less expensive look-alikes. If you happen to have access to both a brand-name item and its look-alike, an interesting experiment is to challenge your friends to guess which is which.

JOIN THE SAVVY SHOPPER GENERATION

Being skeptical, or even suspicious, is a main guideline of smart shopping. We're not talking about paranoia that takes the fun out of buying, but carefulness that keeps you from getting gypped. According to money writer Karen Blumenthal, your generation is "the savviest group of young shoppers ever."[2] You've been marketed to your whole lives and your parents have probably let you make choices since you were little. Nevertheless Blumenthal offers some advice for smart shoppers who want to be even smarter.

Which pair of sunglasses costs $3? Which costs $15? Which costs $117? See answer in appendix.

Don't think you're necessarily getting a good deal when you see that an item is marked down 30 percent (or 50 percent). That kind of drop in price used to mean something, but nowadays many stores inflate the original price so that they can discount quickly and often.

As mentioned earlier, take advantage of "loss leaders," deeply discounted items intended to bring you into the store. The store is willing to take a loss on loss leaders in the hope that you'll buy other merchandise. In addition, watch out for specials, where, for instance, a no-name brand item that resembles a name brand is offered at a big discount.

Whenever you give out information to merchants, you're likely to stay on their mailing lists, e-mail and regular, for a long, long time. If you like that idea, fine. If you find junk mail annoying, be careful what info you share.

Be aware that most stores are trying to make you so comfortable that you'll stay there and keep spending. Try not to get so carried away by music, video screens, murals, and lighting that you lose your good judgment. And if you care about being a smart shopper, think about the mood you're in on a given shopping day. Scientists in a field called behavioral economics have found that if you happen to be angry, fearful, disgusted, or sad, your consumer decision making may be affected. People in a sad mood, for instance, were willing to overpay and undersell.[3] So wait until you're on an even keel to shop until you drop.

HAS THAT PRODUCT BEEN DOCTORED?

As we've already discussed, a cardinal rule of smart shopping is *look at advertisements with a suspicious eye*, especially if ads are slick and expensively produced. A classic example of how advertisers take advantage of us is the doctoring of products in certain TV food commercials. How come that burger looks so glossy and mouth-watering? Because they coated it with Vaseline for the cameras.[4] Although some ads in local newspapers will probably be straightforward, slick network TV commercials should put you on your guard. Most of us are so used to exaggerations in ads that we assume we're not pushovers, but it's smart to ask yourself occasionally, Am I

AM I BEING HAD BY ADS?
Am I being snowed by advertisers who claim their products will make me

- ▶ more popular and accepted?
- ▶ more attractive, desirable, and sexy?
- ▶ more successful and powerful?
- ▶ famous, like the celebrities shown in the ads?
- ▶ carefree, like the models shown on the ski slope or at the beach?

being entertained, flattered, or frightened—and misled—into buying something I don't need? What does the ad promise and what are the odds that the promise will be fulfilled?

SHOPPING ONLINE

One way to cut down on shopping hassles is by taking the online route. If you have already joined, or plan to join, the ranks of online shoppers you'll have lots of company. "Over 34 million kids ages 3 to 17 are online in the United States, representing one-fifth of the total Internet user base. . . . Kids and teens are expected to spend $4.9 billion online in 2005."[5]

For information about super deals on designer clothes, jewelry, electronics, and more, go to sites such as www.undergroundshopper.com.

> "I've bought books online," says Clarissia, age 16, "and it's so easy."
>
> "I buy dolls from Japan on a fairly regular basis," says Alexandra, age 17, "and the service has been nothing short of perfect. The shipping fees are high, but my stuff often arrives after a week, and they're always in excellent condition."

Online Warnings

Not everybody is happy with online shopping. "It's not really worth buying online," says Shaun, age 18. "The process takes forever, and everything seems better online than the actual item you receive."

You'll need to be wary of online ads for quick and easy weight-loss programs and bulletin boards in chat rooms that are advertising in disguise.[6] Tips for avoiding online shopping problems follow.

Make sure a tempting offer is legitimate. Start by shopping at online stores you're familiar with. Be sure the Web address listed in the browser window is what you'd expect it to be— often the store name. If the address looks questionable, the seller may be, too. Check for a physical address and a working phone number, not just a post office box. It's not a bad idea to call the phone number to make sure someone answers.

Look for a certification logo. The Better Business Bureau and TrustE certify and monitor online retailers and take action in the case of fraud. If you're uncertain about a company, contact the Better Business Bureau or a state agency to find out if any complaints have been filed against it. If you have a complaint yourself, get information from wiredsafety.org and/or file a complaint with the Better Business Bureau or the Office of Consumer Affairs.

For online purchases, always pay by credit card instead of a check or debit card. Most credit card companies will reimburse you if you get clipped by Internet fraud.[7]

IF YOU'RE NOT SATISFIED

Okay, whether shopping online or in the mall, what do you do if, once you're home, the designer sweater, pair of skis, digital camera, has a pulled thread, a crack, or a defective lens? Make a complaint. The Better Business Bureau, Consumers Union, and various governmental agencies exist for your protection, but the first move, if you have a gripe, has to be made by you. "It's an easy process," says Crystal, age 17, "if you have the receipt." The Better Business Bureau suggests that you

- complain as soon as possible.
- contact the merchant who sold you the product or service, either by going back to the store or by telephoning. Be prepared to give a clear explanation of your complaint and to describe the product. Have on hand serial number, account number, receipt, cancelled check, or any other papers relating to the purchase. If a salesperson isn't helpful, ask to speak to a supervisor.

Some businesses may ignore complaints unless they're in writing, so if you haven't gotten satisfaction from a return visit or a phone call, write or e-mail the merchant or manufacturer. Include the following in your letter of complaint:

- Your name, address, phone number(s)
- Your account number, if applicable
- A brief explanation of the problem
- The model, make, and serial number, if applicable
- A description of what you have already done to solve the problem
- How you would like the problem resolved
- Copies of all related documents

WHAT IS THE BETTER BUSINESS BUREAU (BBB)?[8] Founded in 1912, this private, nonprofit organization serves both marketers and consumers by promoting honest business. The BBB rates companies on the basis of whether they've gotten customer complaints and how those complaints were settled. Because the BBB isn't a government agency, it's limited to reporting bad business practices to the public and/or to the proper authorities. Most businesses, however, are willing to work with the BBB in resolving disputes. The BBB also reviews local and national charities to help donors make good decisions about giving. And their website provides additional information on truth-in-advertising and consumer and business education.

If your complaint is about a service rather than an item, describe the service and the problem, and give the name of the person who performed the service. If all this fails, contact, at no charge, the Better Business Bureau or the Consumer Protection Agency. Both of these organizations are dedicated to helping you resolve customer dissatisfaction.[9]

Returns

Ordinarily, if you make a complaint to a reliable company, it will replace your merchandise or give you credit. Getting involved with consumer protection groups is usually a last resort. Most merchants want to keep you happy so that you'll come back again. In fact, it's surprisingly easy to return merchandise to large stores if you have complete proof of purchase.

It's a little more complicated to return items to online stores. If you've cracked the plastic wrapper of a CD, video game, tape, or other software, you probably won't be able to send it back. But if you've bought something returnable online from a place like the Gap or Macy's, you can take it to the actual (brick-and-mortar) store—just as if you had bought it there—or you can mail it back. Whether you use the U.S. Postal Service or a private parcel service, it's always smart to insure what you send. United Parcel Service (UPS), for instance, automatically insures up to $100, but if your merchandise is worth more, get extra coverage. You'll probably have to pay the postage on a return, but some companies such as Amazon.com pay for return mailing if your item is defective or if they made an error. Sometimes return forms are included with the packing slip. If not, you can often access the form from the company's website and print it yourself.

It's generally a good idea to call the company first, before you return an item, especially an expensive one. For example, "most sites that sell computers require that you first get a return merchandise authorization (RMA) number from them before you return a computer. Don't, under any circumstances, ship back a computer without first getting this number—otherwise there won't be a record." Some online sellers may accept the return but they'll charge you a restocking fee.[10] A good reason to shop carefully is to avoid the aggravation of sending things back. And regardless of where you buy, do a precheck on the return policy of the seller. Some companies give credit but no refund. Most have a time limit, such as "return within thirty days."

REBATES: WORTH IT OR NOT?

Let's back up a minute. You're buying a computer or some other electronic item. *Rebate* the sign says. Should you favor that brand? First of all, what's a rebate? It's an offer from the manufacturer to send you some money back after your purchase. You must usually mail in a coupon, a receipt, and perhaps a bar code or other proof of purchase. If the manufacturer is reputable, the item is exactly what you want, and you're a fairly patient person, take advantage of the offer. Where do you get the rebate coupons? Sometimes in stores;

A $20-mail-in-rebate is offered at point of purchase in this discount store.

sometimes directly at the point of purchase; or sometimes in newspapers, magazines, or on the Internet. A website called Mr. Rebates offers coupons for more than 500 companies.

Following the rebate directions, you mail in everything the manufacturer asks for, and in some stated amount of time (weeks or months), you should get a check for the promised amount. Are customers always satisfied? No. "The Federal Trade Commission has been investigating complaints about rebate practices since 1998. 'Rebates are a headache,' says Michael Dershowitz, senior attorney. . . . 'Frustrating for consumers and frustrating for us.'"[11]

On the other hand, getting $150 back when you purchase a laptop is well worth the effort. If you do go ahead with a rebate, read the requirements first to make sure you're eligible. Write clearly on the rebate form, using all capital letters. Make copies of everything you mail in, and write down the expected return date. Include in the envelope all documents asked for and consider sending it by registered mail. Use enough postage. And watch carefully for the rebate check so that you don't throw it out with junk mail.

TIPPING

Now let's talk about an expense that often causes confusion—tipping. Also known as a gratuity, a tip is a small sum of money given to someone who performs a service for you. Giving gratuities is an accepted practice around the world, but tipping customs vary depending on the service and the culture.

Who do you tip? In the United States we usually tip restaurant servers, taxi drivers, hair and nail salon workers, porters, and many other workers who receive low basic pay and are expected to make their living from tips. Why tip? To be fair to people who serve you and to insure getting good service when you come back. There are a few situations in which tipping is considered unnecessary or even insulting, but in most cases people who work hard for little salary depend on your tip. In fast-food places where there's no personal service to speak of, you're not expected to leave a gratuity. But in restaurants that offer personal service, tipping is customary, and guidelines can help you decide how much to leave. (Note: A very low tip is often considered worse than none at all. If you don't leave the server a tip, you're said to be "stiffing" him or her.)

What are these guidelines? It's usually considered fair to leave a waiter or waitress between 15 and 20 percent of your total bill (before tax is added on). Fifteen percent is considered the minimum for good service, but if you can afford it and you've gotten great service, you might leave as much as 20 percent. Some restaurants include a service charge in your bill so that you have no choice in the matter of tipping. Others print, right on your bill, the amount the tip would be at various percentages, and it's up to you to decide what percentage to give.

If there's no such information on your bill, you'll have to do the math yourself. If the tax in your state happens to be about 8 percent, it's easy to figure the tip by doubling the tax. Ordinarily you'll round numbers off, to avoid dealing with small change.

Let's say the food, or the service, is awful. Do you still have to tip? If you can make a good case that something is wrong with what you've ordered, make your complaint politely with the server as soon as you notice the problem. If the server is uncooperative, you might ask to speak to the manager. It goes without saying that you'll have to be very tactful to get the problem solved and avoid embarrassment. If your complaint is serious, if you explain politely, and if you're ignored or treated rudely, you're entitled to show dissatisfaction by holding back a tip. On the other hand, stiffing a server, hair stylist, or cab driver without very, very good reason is mean-spirited. Picture yourself in place of the worker, and tip accordingly.

About tipping: If you're lucky enough to have a credit card and you're charging food on it, keep in mind that servers usually appreciate getting their tips in cash. Also, when tipping cab drivers, hair stylists, and others, avoid giving a lot of small change. Although tipping can cause anxiety—Should I have given more? Was that too much?—try not to let it throw you.

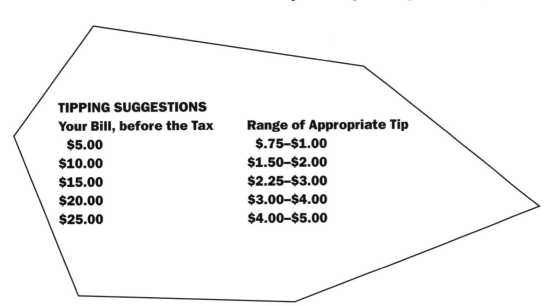

TIPPING SUGGESTIONS

Your Bill, before the Tax	Range of Appropriate Tip
$5.00	$.75–$1.00
$10.00	$1.50–$2.00
$15.00	$2.25–$3.00
$20.00	$3.00–$4.00
$25.00	$4.00–$5.00

For whatever it's worth, even experienced adults are often insecure about tipping.

Okay. You're a smart consumer at the mall. You've mastered buying on the Internet. You can figure percentages of a bill in order to leave a fair tip. What else is there to know, if you're going to get an A+ in shopping? Read on, to find out how to buy big stuff like cell phone service or a car.

NOTES

1. Tere Drenth, *The Everything Budgeting Book* (Avon, MA: Adams Media Corp., 2003), 84.

2. Karen Blumenthal, "Are You Shop-Smart?" *Wall Street Journal Classroom Edition*, December 2004, 19.

3. Sharon Begley, "Heartstrings and Purse Strings," *Wall Street Journal Classroom Edition*, September 2004, 14.

4. Consumer Reports 4Kids, "Food-ad Tricks," n.d., www.zillions.org/Features/Foodadtricks/Food_ad001.html, 1 (accessed February 7, 2006).

5. "Statistics: U.S. Online Shoppers," n.d., www.shop.org/learn/stats_usshop_kids.asp (accessed February 22, 2006).

6. "Scams and Fraud," n.d., www.wiredsafety.org/scams_fraud/advertising.html, 3 (accessed February 22, 2006).

7. Kelly Spors, "Tips for Safe Online Shopping," *Wall Street Journal Classroom Edition*, February 2005, 5.

8. "Better Business Bureau," *Wikipedia*, en.wikipedia.org/wiki/Better_business_bureau (accessed February 12, 2006).

9. "Consumer Complaints," n.d., www.atg.wa.gov/consumer/complain.shtml (accessed January 2, 2007).

10. Preston Gralla, "Shopping: Returning Items Bought Online," *Access Magazine*, January 2, 2000, 16.

11. Jennie Phipps, "Consumers Getting Clipped by Some Rebates," Bankrate.com, July 23, 2003, www.bankrate.com/brm/news/advice/20030723a1.asp, 1 (accessed July 27, 2005).

11 Ring Tones and Dream Machines: Cell Phone Plans and Car Purchases

DO YOU NEED A CELL PHONE?

Maybe you're among the 7 out of 10 kids (age 16 or 17) who already have a cell phone. The numbers are lower for younger kids, but "cell phone ownership among U.S. teens 13–17 grew by 43 percent in the past year, with teen girls (61 percent) more likely to carry them than teen boys (46 percent). And daily cell phone usage has more than doubled in the past year."[1] Forty percent of the earth's population will be carrying cell phones by 2009.[2] If you aren't yet flipping your phone lid, the odds are that you will be some day soon. So, how crucial is it to have one?

"I don't have a cell phone," says Alexandra, age 17. "Minutes, rates, charges. It's way too complicated for me." A lot of adults think cell phones are just one more example of kids being spoiled. "It's my life," says Crystal, age 17, of her phone. "I can't go anywhere without it because I feel weird." Almost nobody argues that cell phones are useful for keeping safe. And, of course, they're convenient. You call if you need a ride, or you call to say you have a ride, so your parents don't need to pick you up. It's cell phone overuse and those unpredictable bills that cause parents to groan.

"I use it more than I should," Mariany, age 18, reports. "At first the bills were astronomical. Luckily my dad gave me unlimited text messages on the family plan, and that's only $10 extra a month."

"My bill sometimes comes out to about $300 for no apparent reason," says Shaun, age18. Assuming that you need,

Do you need a cell phone?

want, and are permitted to have a cell phone, how do you go about choosing the right deal?

According to tech writer David Pogue, "Most people correctly consider the traditional cellular plan to be insanely complex. Every month's bill is a shock, because the cellphone companies make it extraordinarily difficult to keep track of how many of your monthly 'anytime minutes' you have used up."[3] For this reason and others, users are often dissatisfied. According to *Consumer Reports* magazine, 35 percent of cell phone subscribers changed carriers in 2005.[4]

How to Get the Best Deal

To be a satisfied customer, what should you check out before you sign up? First, check coverage and reception. What good is your phone if it doesn't work? J. D. Power and Associates ranks major carriers in each region. Point.com is another website to use for research. From these and other online and offline sources, and from people you know who have cell phones, find out which service is most reliable in your area. Second, of course, compare prices—easier said than done.

Financial correspondent Vera Gibbons says that major carriers basically offer the same plans, but they're in fierce competition with each other and are always offering new deals. According to one survey, 45 percent of teenagers with cell phones are part of a family plan. Adding a user is ordinarily only an extra $9.99 a month. You can save a lot if you combine a family plan with free in-network calling, or mobile-to-mobile calling. Being able to call home, or call family members, for free is great for customers. Of course, your family still has to stay within its allotted monthly minutes for nonfamily calls.[5]

If you're getting your own service, apart from your family, it's important to examine your phone habits before you select a plan. "Most people have no idea how many minutes they use each month," Gibbons says. "They may be going over their limits—and paying steep fees—or only using a fraction of the minutes they pay for." She recommends buying a plan with slightly more minutes than you expect to use, in order to avoid overuse fees.[6] Some other advice includes the following:

- ◎ If you go with one carrier and then see a better plan advertised, negotiate with your carrier. It may give you the same deal.

- ◎ Since the coolest, newest phones often come with very specific (expensive) plans, consider taking a phone that the carrier gives away free.

- ◎ Use the ring tones and games that come with your phone instead of expensive extras. You'll lower your cost.

- ◎ Take advantage of plans that give you unlimited nighttime and weekend calling. Night usually means 9 p.m. to 6 a.m. So whenever possible, make your calls in free time. Some companies consider night to be after 7 p.m.

- ◎ Read patiently about the special features that various carriers offer. Plans with rollovers let you save leftover minutes from

month to month. Some plans offer free incoming calls. A regional carrier may offer unlimited calls at a low price, but if you make calls out of your region you'll get badly hit.

- **Avoid using directory assistance, which costs a dollar or more.**
- **Find out how to access your account online, or on the phone itself, so that you can check frequently to see how many minutes you have left for that month.**
- **Be aware that carriers are required to give you time to test your phone, usually 14 days, so if you're not pleased with your service, you can get out of the contract.[7]**

"Another way to avoid ugly surprises when you open your bill," says David Pogue, "pay in advance. Prepaid plans are popular among those on a budget because there are no age limits, contracts, annual commitments, overuse charges or even monthly bills. Instead you buy minutes in advance, either on a Web page or at a convenience store. The trouble with this method is that the per-minute cost is high."[8]

Further Warnings

If you're someone who has trouble keeping track of possessions, it might be worth insuring your phone in case you lose it.

You may find negotiating with carriers to be the easiest part of cell phone ownership. Hassling with parents over who-pays-what may turn out to be the worst. "I use my phone, under my parents' service, a lot," says Matt, age 17. "The cost issues aren't with my calls but with my text messaging. I never know how many minutes I've used. My parents charge me the extra. I've had to pay $12 some months, but I have friends who've had to pay $500."

Text Messaging

What is behind these huge bills? Aha!—text messaging, also known as SMS, or Short Message Service. It's the service that enables you to communicate from a place where you can't call or can't hear. It allows you to instant-message. Through SMS you can get customized information, such as sports scores; talk with a group of people all at once; or order ring tones. Since the first text message was sent on December 3, 1992, people have been using this service more and more. "By mid-2004 texts were being sent at a rate of 500 billion messages per annum."[9] That's twice as many as in 2001. Text messages in the United States cost about 10¢ each, so if you see yourself as a frequent texter, look into plans that allow you to send unlimited messages.

Read the fine print to verify what you're paying to instant-message.

Cell Phone Fraud

As if huge cell phone bills aren't enough to worry about, another thing to keep you awake at night is the possibility of cell phone fraud. Fraud occurs when somebody signs up for service with, let's say—to complete the nightmare—*your* personal information. How did they get your name, address, and Social Security number? By stealing them in the same way thieves steal credit card information. When you buy anything in a store or on the Internet, keep ID data as private as possible, and if you get bills for calls you didn't make, report fraud immediately to your cell phone carrier.

CARS

Okay, cell phone plans can be expensive but they're peanuts compared to cars. Whole books, magazines, newspapers, and websites are devoted to car buying, so we'll take only a brief look at this vast subject here.

"Your own car," Karen Blumenthal says, "freedom from carpools and parents' schedules. . . . Unfortunately . . . you'll quickly find that a car is one of the biggest financial burdens out there."[10]

Sources of Info on Cars

Do research to learn your options and to be well-informed when you meet the car salesperson. Websites such as Kelley Blue Book.com, cars.com, and Edmunds.com provide you with the price ranges of new and used cars. Pictures and comparisons may help you narrow down your choice.

BE ECONOMICAL AND SAFE, TOO
1. Consider a used car. They're cheaper and getting a dent will be less awful. (But if you aren't a good car mechanic, expect to pay for repairs along the way.)
2. If you buy a used car, choose a fairly recent model with up-to-date safety features. Check out the National Highway Transportation Safety Administration's website to see results of their tests (www.safecar.gov).
3. Consider the size of the car. If you're in a collision, the smaller car is almost always at a disadvantage.

Another source of car-buying help is current magazines such as *Consumer Reports* or *U.S. News & World Report*, the latter of which contains Richard J. Newman's list of the 10 safest and cheapest cars for teens. Based on his research, Newman ruled out compacts, subcompacts, and SUVs for safety reasons. The cars he chose all cost less than $15,000; got at least 20 miles per gallon; and scored high in crash tests.[11] For prices you can't beat, Toyota, Honda, Nissan, and other manufacturers are offering newly designed subcompact models for under $13,000.

Leases

Another possibility is leasing a car. Leasing is a sort of long-term rental. Depending on the exact deal, you either return the car at the end of the lease or buy it at the current value. The advantage of leasing is paying less money up front, although you may pay slightly more in the long run. As in most financial matters, if you're a minor, you'll have to go through your parents to arrange a lease.

Coming Up with the Bucks

Once you've found the best car for the money, how do you pay for this dream machine? Maybe you've saved up the total amount. Or maybe it's a present from grandparents. Great, but very likely not true. Consider whether parents or grandparents would be willing, however, to give you a loan at a favorable rate. Otherwise you'll need to take out a commercial loan. See chapter 12 on borrowing for additional information, but here's some car-loan advice:

About half of vehicle buyers go straight to the dealer, says Kerry Rivera of Toyota Financial Services. The advantage is convenient, one-stop shopping.[12] But you don't have to finance your car that way. Find out if your own bank or credit union offers a lower rate than the dealer.

Borrowing for a Car

Do you have a credit rating? Even if you don't have a credit score, surely your parents do, and if they're cosigning with you for a car loan, the lender will care about their score. Car buyers who have good credit ratings can borrow at a lower rate than buyers with a poor credit record. For example, "on a four-year loan of $14,000, the buyer with poor credit will pay $380 a month, or $58 a month more than the buyer with good credit. Over four years, that amounts to $2,784 in added interest."[13] In short, with a good credit rating you can borrow at a lower rate. Remember, of course, that interest rates are subject to change.

Regardless of the rate, however, the longer the period of your loan the more interest you'll pay, so it may be worth paying more each month to end the loan sooner. "The average new-car loan runs over five years, according to a 2004 survey by Power Information Network. Younger buyers tend to opt for long loan terms—up to seven years."[14] Blumenthal advises kids to take a maximum four-year loan on a used car.[15]

It's possible to get car loans online these days. And even if you're not eligible to get a loan on your own, check out Internet websites anyway. You can learn a lot about comparative rates for car loans on sites such as eloan.com and Bankrate.com.

Making Sure You Don't Get a Lemon

If you're thinking of buying a used car, prepare to check it out: body condition, tires, suspension, engine condition, exhaust system, and more. If you aren't an expert yourself, take a knowledgeable person with you. In advance consult books or articles such as "How to Inspect a Used Car."[16]

"Beware of finance companies that guarantee loans to anyone, regardless of credit problems, income, or past histories. These companies are taking a risk with their money, and they usually charge higher interest on their loans than a bank or credit union."[17]

Consider a used car.

Ongoing Car Expenses

Once the car is yours, expenses will start mounting. Insurance. Gulp. Gas. Gulp, gulp. Repairs and tolls. Gulp, gulp, gulp. If you're wondering why teenagers get clobbered by insurance rates, consider that 16- to 19-year-old drivers are four times more likely to get into an accident than older drivers. The highest insurance rates are paid by male drivers under 25. With the increase in young female drivers in the last 20 years, however, the accident rates between the genders are evening out.[18]

There are ways to save on car insurance, however.

1. **Get on your parents' policy, if possible. Their insurance bill may escalate greatly, but it will still be cheaper that way.**

2. Look for discounts, as much as 25 percent for maintaining at least a B average. Obviously, insurers have figured out that kids with good grades are safer drivers.

3. If you live in a state that gives discounts for experience in driving, take advantage of it. The experience may be a formal course or hours logged in with an experienced driver.

4. Drive an insurance-friendly vehicle—one that has airbags and other safety features and isn't a target for thieves.

5. Compare prices from different insurance companies to get the best deal.

And after you have the insurance, drive carefully—and sober. "Death and injury are the highest price drivers pay from drinking and driving, but even if you manage to survive, a D.U.I. ticket will cost teenagers big time. As a teen driver, you'll likely be cancelled and if you can get insurance, expect to pay a much higher rate for the next 3–5 years. . . . Rack up more than three crashes and/or citations and you'll face cancellation or non-renewal."[19]

Let's hope that if you want a car as a teenager you'll get one, but if a car doesn't come your way until later, take consolation from the thought that you'll have more money now to spend on other things.

NOTES

1. John Consoli, "Teen Cell Subs Heavy TV Users," *Mediaweek*, May 3, 2005, www.mediaweek.com/mw/search/article_display .jsp?vnu_content_id=1000904910 (accessed February 26, 2006).

2. David Pogue, "1 Landline + 1 Cellphone = 1 Handset," *New York Times*, August 4, 2005, E1.

3. David Pogue, "Tough Course: The Calculus of Cellphones," *New York Times*, August 3, 2005, E1.

4. CBS News, "Become a Happier Cell Phone Owner," March 10, 2005, www.cbsnews.com/stories/2005/03/10/earlyshow/living/money/main679246.shtml, 1 (accessed February 27, 2006).

5. CBS News, "Become a Happier Cell Phone User," 2.

6. CBS News, "Become a Happier Cell Phone User," 2–3.

7. CBS News, "Become a Happier Cell Phone User," 2–3.

8. Pogue, "Tough Course," E1.

9. "Short Message Service," *Wikipedia*, en.wikipedia.org/wiki/ Short_message_service (accessed March 1, 2006).

10. Karen Blumenthal, "Freedom Isn't Free," *Wall Street Journal Classroom Edition*, April 2005, 16.

11. *U.S. News & World Report*, December 12, 2005, 57.

12. Christina Uss, "Beginner's Guide to Car Loan Hunting," *Young Money*, March/April 2005, 18.

13. Blumenthal, "Freedom Isn't Free," 16.

14. Uss, "Beginner's Guide," 18.

15. Blumenthal, "Freedom Isn't Free," 16.

16. Bob Elliston, "How to Inspect a Used Car," *Young Money*, May/June 2006, 18–19.

17. Susan Shelly, *The Complete Idiot's Guide to Money for Teens* (Indianapolis, IN: Alpha Books, 2001), 145.

18. Rocky Mountain Insurance Information Association, "Teens Shopping for Auto Insurance," n.d., www.rmiia.org/Auto/Teens/ Buying_Auto_Insurance.htm (accessed March 2, 2006).

19. Rocky Mountain Insurance Information Association, "Teens Shopping for Auto Insurance."

12 Getting the Credit: Debit and Credit Cards

You're eight years old and you want some junk at the dollar store. You borrow a couple of bucks from an older sibling, who's shrewd enough to make you pay an extra dollar as a penalty. Now you're a young adult, however,

> "I have a credit card and pay more than the minimum payment each month. However I have friends who are in *big* trouble because of credit cards. One of my friends owes over $8,000. It is just too easy to charge."—Andrea, age 19
>
> "I had no idea how much that little plastic card would mess up my life. I got my first credit card offer in the mail when I was 16 years old."—Kristin, age 16[1]

and the stakes are higher. You buy more expensive things and the penalty is called interest. Relatives and friends may still be willing to lend to you, with or without interest, but chances are you'll soon be borrowing money one way or another from strangers who work for banks or loan companies.

ARE YOU READY TO BORROW?

Maybe you're doing just fine and have no desire or need to borrow at this time, but almost everybody borrows at some point in life—for an education, a car, or an apartment or house.

The ideal situation is to borrow only when you're confident about meeting payments and when the value and benefits of what you buy outweigh the stress of paying bills. So if you're struggling to make ends meet, is it a good idea to borrow—to get involved with a credit card? Not unless you have enough secure income to meet monthly payments.

Let's assume, though, that you have a checking account and maybe an ATM card that allows you to draw money from that account. The question is, will you benefit by adding a debit or a credit card to your wallet?

First let's clarify the difference between the two kinds of cards.

DEBIT CARDS

A debit card, issued by a bank, allows you to pay for purchases (and take out cash) from your checking or savings account. With a credit card, on the other hand, the bank is paying, temporarily, for whatever you buy—up to a certain limit. You sign an agreement that you'll pay a minimum amount when you get the bill, plus interest on whatever you hold over from month to month.

Why have a debit card? For safety and convenience, so that you won't need to carry a lot of cash. Debit cards, with their higher degree of control, also provide good training for having a credit card. Nevertheless, there are disadvantages and complications even with debit cards. For instance, if you lose any kind of card—or if it gets stolen—the card finder may use it, which creates aggravation and sometimes actual loss of your funds.

PREPAID CREDIT CARDS

As we've already said, credit cards generally require no money deposited up front. An exception is the prepaid credit card, or secured card, which is sometimes offered to new customers or ones who've had past problems with credit. The prepaid credit card needs to be loaded with funds, which it then draws from when you use the card to make a purchase. The prepaid credit card may have the advantage of being accepted even more widely than a debit card. Both the debit card and prepaid credit card hold the card owner to a spending limit.[2] If the prepaid card is "reloadable," money can be added at any point. Prepaid cards are good self-control mechanisms, if you're a person who spends impulsively.

Prepaid cards are sometimes given as gifts. The benefit of being given a prepaid credit card rather than gift card to Macy's, let's say, is that you aren't limited to any one store.

Prepaid cards sound economical and safe, right? Be wary, though, even if the card has a low, paid-up-front limit. Read the fine print of the bank's terms and conditions. You'll probably be hit with a card activation fee; a shipping and handling fee; a monthly maintenance fee; and extra fees if you talk to a service agent on the phone, order a paper statement, make cash withdrawals, or lose and have to replace your card. The Motley Fool says, in a typical case, "Junior's racked up $23.90 on the card before he's even headed to Tower Records."[3]

There are other things to watch out for. Unless you keep a cushion of money in your account ($100 perhaps), you might find, when your balance is low, that your card is declined. Not to mention that these cards expire. That means you pay a new fee each year, and "Industry experts say up to 17% of balances on loadable and nonreloadable cards typically go unused."[4] In other words, people lose money by letting the card age out with some of their money still in the bank.

If you and your parents decide that some type of debit or credit card (prepaid or otherwise) is in your best interest, you'll have to sift through a ton of offers in the mail, in the media, and on the Internet. "Prepaid debit cards for teens are one of the fastest-growing segments for Visa, MasterCard, Discover, and American Express. According to TowerGroup, bank-issued gift cards will reach $300 billion in sales next year."[5] By the way, let's emphasize *parents or guardians*, regardless of which kind of card we're talking about. If you're under 18, you'll need them to cosign or to add you to their credit or debit card account. This practice is common. One mother writing to a

Credit card images displayed at an ATM.

parental-advice website says, "My daughters both were on our credit cards since age 14 and it worked very well. We can tell which postings are theirs. . . . The groundrule that the account is to be paid off each month set a good habit in place."[6]

CHOOSING A CARD

So how to choose a particular debit card or credit card? As always, watch out for misleading or sneaky advertising. Read the terms carefully and be skeptical of the celebrity sell. Just as idols often appear in magazine and TV ads, they may crop up not only hawking a card in a commercial but also looking up at you from your card when you open your wallet. Type in "teen debit card or credit card offers" on an Internet search engine and you'll see dozens of possibilities. Compare them in terms of details such as fees, how you add cash, number of retail locations where you can use the card, safety features, and reward points. Get help from your parents and/or other experienced adults.

ADVANTAGES OF PLASTIC

If debit cards and prepaid credit cards are safer in terms of keeping you within your budget, why even think about getting a regular credit card? Because they're useful in emergencies, and as long as you can pay your bill at the end of the month, there's no interest involved. Transactions you may want to make someday, such as purchasing on the Internet, renting a car, or booking a hotel room, are much easier with a credit card. For roughly 60 million Americans without bank accounts, living without cards is getting harder: "'You're effectively locked out of the American Dream if you don't have some kind of plastic, and it's going to get worse,' says Russell Simmons, the hip-hop mogul, whose Rushcard lets holders put their paychecks onto plastic."[7]

Another advantage of cards, both debit and credit, is that they're a forced way of keeping a record of your purchases, since everything you charge on the card will appear on your

HOW DID CREDIT CARDS START?
Once upon a time, people bartered goods. Then they used shells. Eventually they paid with coins and paper. The idea of charging purchases got started after World War II, when department stores and gas stations gave credit in order to build customer loyalty. Then in 1950 several businessmen got together to create the Diners Club card, which enabled consumers to use one card for multiple purchases. The idea caught on so well that now, more than 50 years later, 144 million Americans have general purpose credit cards.[8] The typical American household has eight credit cards, with total family debt of $7,500.[9]

monthly statement. Some credit card companies send you a year-end summary, with your expenses listed by category, a record that helps you budget for the year to come. Credit cards are also an aid in learning to manage money because they test your ability to pay bills on time each month. If you pass the test, you'll find it easier to borrow bigger sums in the future—for education, cars, or real estate.

TEENAGERS AND CARDS

Teenagers have been admitted more recently to the card club. According to the student loan company Nellie Mae, 81 percent

WHAT'S A CREDIT RATING?[10]
A credit rating is a score that helps lenders decide if you're a good risk or not. The rating, determined by a credit bureau, is based on information about your identity and your borrowing history. How many, and what kind of, accounts do you have? How long have you had them? Have you paid all bills on time? Are there any late payments, collection actions, or outstanding debts?

Obviously you won't have a credit rating until you've started borrowing. One reason for opening an account and applying for a credit card is to help you establish this rating. A good score will affect your getting loans for biggies like cars and home mortgages. Future jobs and insurance premiums can also be influenced by your credit rating.

of college freshmen have at least one card.[11] And "the average undergraduate today owes some $2,100, spread out over more than four credit cards."[12] The effort to get more and younger teens to sign up is continually intensifying, so if you haven't received an offer yet, look for one in the mail soon. Credit card companies send out about 6 billion letters a year.[13]

Stories of kids overspending on cards are common. You've probably heard tales from friends, seen them in magazines, or tuned into *Oprah* when the young adult guests are explaining how they racked up $50,000 debts. So don't be surprised if your parents hesitate to cosign with you. Because charging on a card is easy and doesn't seem like spending real money, lots of teens get into a mess.

BAD CREDIT SCENARIO[14]
"The $500 limit seemed like a lot of money," says Kristin Nemsick, "but I had a part-time job, so I felt OK about charging things. I looked at it this way: as long as I could manage $20 a month, I could buy what I wanted, on the spot. It almost seemed too good to be true. And it was.

"I started shopping up a storm and went nuts ordering catalogs. . . . Before I knew it, more credit card offers came in the mail. All I had to do was forge one of my parent's signatures, and within six months I had a total of four cards with different limits. I figured I could pay another $40 or so a month to my creditors and continue buying. By the time I was 17, I owed almost $3,000. I couldn't understand how it added up so quickly until I realized finance charges were tacked onto the bill. . . . I was actually paying almost double for everything."

In "Bad Credit Scenario" Kristin, luckily—with support from a grandmother and her own hard work over several years—paid off her debts and got back on track. In a few extreme cases, no one was able to save out-of-control teenagers, who ended up committing suicide for reasons related to debt.[15] Let's hope you're thinking, "Not me." And let's hope you're right.

PREMIUM CREDIT CARDS

You, let's say, are in the cautious and responsible majority. For safety, convenience, and chalking up experience—and with the blessing of your family—you're going to get a credit card. What kind? We've already discussed secured cards that require an up-front deposit. This kind will be easiest to get if you're just starting out. Then there's the regular, or general purpose, credit card, which does not require a deposit. Finally, there are premium cards (gold, platinum, titanium), which have higher limits and extra features, such as product warranties, travel insurance, or emergency services.[16]

Your credit limit, by the way, is the maximum total amount, including purchases, cash advances, balance transfers, fees, and finance charges, that you're allowed to charge on your card. If you go over this limit, you will probably have to pay an extra fee.

What's the story with free airplane miles and other stuff that certain credit cards offer? They make those offers because they want your business. They want you now, and they hope to hold on to you forever. Visa and MasterCard are "joint ventures owned by the thousands of banks that issue cards under those names."[17] These banks make money from the interest you pay and from commissions that merchants pay them (1 to 5 percent of each transaction).

There is stiff competition among banks, which is why they offer you extras like rebates (money back), airplane miles, car rental insurance, and registration in case your card is lost or stolen. If you go for a card that gives cash rebates, by the way, avoid ones with "spending tiers." These reward you for spending a lot. Find a card with a flat rebate percentage, so that "from the very first dollar spent to the last, you'll always receive the same rebate percentage."[18] Note that cards with extra features often cost more in fees and interest, so consider getting the most basic type.

If and when you get a credit card, think of every purchase as a loan from a bank. Even if you pay off your card in full at the end of each month, technically you're buying with borrowed money.[19]

READING THE FINE PRINT

Here's another bit of advice from experts: compare interest rates carefully. Credit cards are the most expensive kind of debt, more expensive than car and home loans, because they aren't backed by an asset like a car or home—just by your word that you're going to pay your bill. Credit card companies hope you *won't* pay off monthly. They hope you'll pay only the minimum each month, because that's how they make the most profit. Seventy percent of their revenue comes from the high interest you pay if you send in the minimum and "roll over" the rest.

So if you expect to carry over a balance from month to month, look for the card with the lowest interest rate (stated as an annual percentage rate, or APR). Notice that a single credit card may have several APRs. You'll pay a higher rate for cash advances than for purchases of goods. Interest rates may also increase over time or if you make a payment late. Also, check whether the annual rate is fixed or variable. Even fixed rates change sometimes, but not as often as variables.

If interest rates aren't so important because you expect to pay off your bill at the end of each month, choose a card that offers benefits that are especially valuable to you. The ideal card will be one with no annual fee and a longer grace period (length of time to pay off before you get a finance charge). Also, avoid taking cash advances on your card because the fees can be very costly.

Okay, you're going to join the cardholders club. How do you go about choosing? Look at offers in the mail, addressed to you or your parents. Check out ads in newspapers and magazines. Again, the Internet is probably the best source of current information. Type in "credit card" and you'll find lists of plans, rates, and terms to compare. The Federal Reserve System surveys credit card companies every six months, so federalreserve.gov is a good place to check.

Under federal law, all solicitations and applications for credit cards must include certain key information. It's up to you to check out details on such matters as APRs, variable rate info, grace period length, method of computing balance, annual fees, minimum finance charge, and other fees (transaction for cash advances, balance-transfer, late fee, and over-the-limit fee).[20] "It has gotten to the point where the fine print is becoming almost outright abusive of customers," says Michael Shames, executive director of a consumer advocacy group.[21] Of course it's a pain to pore over the fine print, but you may be sorry if you don't.

KEEPING GOOD RECORDS

Now you've chosen a card, gotten a cosigner if necessary, read the terms, and signed an agreement. What else should you be aware of as the owner of a credit card? Hold on to your receipts so you can compare them with your statement when it comes. If you let receipts get out of your hands, anybody can use them as sources of information about your account. When you're ready to dispose of receipts, tear them up before you toss them. And if you spot an error on the statement—that is, if you're charged for something you didn't buy—follow the bank's instructions for protesting a charge.

When it comes time to pay your monthly bill, you have two options. You can write a check and mail it to the card company or you can pay your bill online. In the latter case, you arrange with your bank to have your monthly credit card charge deducted automatically from your checking account. This method is safe and quick and saves the cost of checks and postage. Some people pay all, or most, of their bills online.

CREDIT CARD SECURITY

Another thing to arrange is how to keep your card safe—that is, how not to lose it, have it stolen, or have it otherwise used by an unauthorized person. Here are a few tips:

- Always keep the card in the same place, logically, in your wallet.
- Put the card back immediately after a purchase, and be more watchful than ever of your wallet.
- Make a photocopy of your card along with the phone number of the issuer, and keep this copy separate from the card.

Losing cash is unpleasant enough, but losing your card leaves you vulnerable to liability for purchases made by somebody else.

If you lose an ATM, debit, or credit card, however, don't panic too much. Federal laws and bank policies limit your responsibility, as long as you take action right away. "If you notify the card issuer within a reasonable time after you discover the loss or theft, usually 30 days, you're not responsible for any charges made after the notification. For charges made before the notification, you'll be liable for only $50 (many credit card issuers waive even this small charge)."[22] Acting quickly is especially important when ATM and debit cards are lost. If you don't notify the bank fast enough, you may be liable for a substantial amount.

When you call to report a lost card, you'll ordinarily be told to expect a replacement card in the mail. This card will have a different number, so if you've been having any payments deducted automatically from your card, you'll need to inform those companies of your new number.

Losing a card because you've been careless is annoying and time consuming. Having a card stolen will probably raise your temperature. But worse than either of these misfortunes is being the victim of identity theft. That is, your card is in your wallet, but somebody's draining your checking account and/or running up bills on your credit card.

139

IDENTITY THEFT

How are they doing it? They're phishing, pronounced "fishing," and that's exactly what these pirates are doing— fishing for your personal financial information. They want your account numbers, passwords, Social Security numbers, and other private information. With the confidential information they steal from you, these thieves try to take out loans or get credit cards or driver's licenses in your name. They can harm your financial reputation, and the trouble can go on for years.[23] The way these phishers get what they want is by setting up phony websites that look like the real ones you deal with. They may e-mail you, claiming they need verification of, or an update on, your personal information (Social Security

---

HOW TO PROTECT YOURSELF FROM IDENTITY THEFT

Don't give out personal information over the phone or Internet unless you're positive you know who you're dealing with.

Q: What kind of personal information?

A: Social Security number, account numbers, passwords, mother's maiden name, and the like.

Q: What's the danger?

A: Someone getting information from you could pretend to be you. He or she could charge items or withdraw money from your account.

Q: If I have to do business on the phone, how can I be sure I'm talking to an authorized person?

A: Initiate the call yourself. *Don't call me, I'll call you!* It's not a bad idea to take your business to a credit union or local bank branch, where you recognize the voices of employees and they recognize yours.

Q: What else can I do to make sure no one charges the Brooklyn Bridge to me?

A: Review account statements when they arrive to make sure they're accurate. If a statement is late, call the financial institution to ask why. If you can access your statement online, check it out frequently and if you're charged for a bridge, report it immediately.

number, place of birth, your mother's maiden name). Then they use the personal info to get your money or charge to your card.

How common a problem is identity theft? A 2003 survey showed that 27.3 million Americans have been victims of identity theft in the last five years, including 9.9 million people in that year alone. Victims reported that these thefts cost them $5 billion. Approximately 5 million people in that year discovered the thefts by themselves, and about 2.5 million people were alerted by their card companies. Some people didn't realize they were victims until they applied for credit and got turned down.[24]

What to Do about Identity Theft

If you realize that somebody has been into your accounts, contact your financial institution right away. You can find the necessary phone number on your monthly statement, in a phone book, or on the Internet. As mentioned earlier, it's helpful to make a copy of your card and record the phone number for emergencies. Also, if you suspect that you've been had, report your suspicion to the Federal Trade Commission by calling 1-877-IDTHEFT or at www.consumer.gov/idtheft. Information on that website tells you exactly how to proceed.

Even if it seems as if problems outweigh the benefits of owning a credit card, you'll probably find, if you're careful, that the opposite is true.

NOTES

1. Kristin Nemsick, "Credit Cards Ruined My Life," *Teen*, May 1999, 84.

2. Dayana Yochim, "Should You Drive Your Teen into Debit?" The Motley Fool, September 28, 2004, www.fool.com/news/commentary/2004/commentary04092804.htm, 2 (accessed March 2, 2006).

3. Yochim, "Should You Drive Your Teen into Debt?" 3.

4. Yochim, "Should You Drive Your Teen into Debt?" 3.

5. Yochim, "Should You Drive Your Teen into Debt?" 1.

6. UCB Parents Advice about Teenagers, "Credit Card for Teens," parents.berkeley.edu/advice/teens/creditcard.html (accessed March 7, 2006).

7. Jathon Sapsford, "The Power of Plastic," *Wall Street Journal Classroom Edition*, November 2004, 8.

8. Sapsford, "Power of Plastic," 8.

9. Patrick McGeehan, "Soaring Interest Compounds Credit Card Pains for Millions," November 21, 2004, www.richmond.edu/~bmayes/pdf/Credit%20Cards_The%20Plastic%20Trap.pdf (accessed January 2, 2007).

10. Rebecca Lindsey, "Credit Cards 101: A Student's Guide to Credit Cards," *Young Money*, November/December 2004, 4.

11. Lindsey, "Credit Cards 101," 4.

12. Paul J. Lim, "Kid Stuff," *U.S. News & World Report*, December 12, 2005, 56.

13. Damon Darlin, "Gift Horses to Consider: Credit Cards That Reward," *New York Times*, December 31, 2005, sec. C.1.

14. Nemsick, "Credit Cards Ruined My Life," 84.

15. Marjolijn Bijlefeld and Sharon K. Zoumbaris, *Teen Guide to Personal Financial Management* (Westport, CT: Greenwood Press, 2000), 1.

16. Federal Reserve Board, "Choosing a Credit Card," n.d., www.federalreserve.gov/pubs/shop/, 5 (accessed May 5, 2005).

17. Sapsford, "Power of Plastic," 8.

18. Darin Shebesta, "Are Rebate Cards Right for You?" *Young Money*, September/October 2004, 6.

19. Karen Blumenthal, "Play Your Cards Right," *Wall Street Journal Classroom Edition*, November 2004, www.wsjclassroomedition.com/archive/04nov/cons_ednov.htm (accessed January 2, 2007).

20. Blumenthal, "Play Your Cards Right."

21. Michael Shames quoted in McGeehan, "Soaring Interest."

22. Nolo, "Your Liability If You Lose Your ATM, Debit, or Credit Card," n.d., www.nolo.com/article.cfm/ObjectID/36CE716A-D287-414B-992B6EFC72E4557A/c (accessed March 9, 2006).

23. "How to Stop Identity Theft," *Young Money*, March/April 2005, 16.

24. Federal Trade Commission, "FTC Releases Survey of Identity Theft in U.S.," September 3, 2003, www.ftc.gov/opa/2003/09/idtheft.htm (accessed April 4, 2006).

13 Enrolling in Money: Becoming Financially Literate

Are you convinced by now that it's smart to understand money matters? No matter how much you already know, you'll need to keep refreshing your brain if you want to be up-to-date. The two basic ways to keep learning are through formal courses and clubs, and through informal means—that is, teaching yourself.

ARE YOU LEARNING ABOUT MONEY AT HOME?

An obvious place to learn about money matters informally is in your own family. Maybe you've been lucky enough to have received homeschooling right from the start. A JumpStart poll of more than 4,000 students in 33 states shows that 58.3 percent of the kids polled said they're learning money skills at home, as opposed to 19.5 percent who are learning at school, and 17.6 percent from experience.[1]

Meanwhile a Harris Poll shows that although kids say they want money advice from their parents, over half of those surveyed say they receive little or none. The ones who did get money-management advice report getting more from mothers or stepmothers than from fathers or stepfathers. And girls, especially, tend to trust advice from mothers more than advice from fathers. (A possible explanation is the number of teens living in households headed by women.) Some kids also report getting money advice from grandparents and other family members.[2]

Some studies show that teens and parents aren't always on the same wavelength when it comes to financial discussions. For instance, one survey indicates that more than 70 percent of parents said they talked to their teens about credit cards, but only 44 percent of teens said they had been talked to by parents on that subject. In other words, they may be talking but you may not be listening. Or else parents aren't reporting things right.[3]

If your family is talking to you, listen. And if your family isn't talking, think about initiating a discussion yourself. Participating is often the best way to learn, so if your family members are approachable, find out if they'll let you

- sit with them when they pay their bills;
- watch them go over budgets or bank statements;
- go to work with a parent or sibling;
- be involved in grocery shopping for a week or more;
- participate in the decision to buy a major appliance or car; or
- go with them to a stockbroker or bank.[4]

Not all parents are going to be comfortable with telling you about their money dealings. If you ask politely and they react negatively, you may have no choice except to look elsewhere for information.

The good news is that more high schools are offering courses in personal finance these days. Maybe this is a result of the statistic that 65.5 percent of 12th graders got failing grades in a recent nationwide JumpStart survey of financial knowledge. In any case, "at least eight states have made personal financial education a required course. The states include Idaho, Illinois, Georgia, Kansas, Kentucky, New York, Texas, and Utah."[5] And in 2004, 24 state bills, resolutions, and proclamations were introduced in Congress in attempts to improve financial literacy through public education.[6]

Let's hope you're lucky enough to go to a school that offers a range of business courses. For example, Teaneck High School in New Jersey (with about 1,200 students) runs four or five sections of Financial Planning each year. The following electives are also available to juniors and seniors: Young Entrepreneurs,

Dynamics of Business, Introduction to Accounting, Computer Accounting, Investments, Marketing Essentials, and Advanced Projects in Marketing. This list is longer than the list of business courses offered by some colleges, and Teaneck High provides business clubs as well, as part of the extracurricular program.

If your school doesn't offer these courses now, it may add them in the future. Organizations such as the JumpStart Coalition, Junior Achievement, and the National Endowment for Financial Education are all working hard to develop and publish materials, offer advice and support to teachers, measure financial literacy, give awards, sponsor competitions, and publicize their agendas in schools. JumpStart operates on contributions from dozens of companies. Junior Achievement, based in Colorado Springs, Colorado, gets contributions from individuals and businesses and receives help from volunteers. One project it sponsors involves publicizing the World Bank International Essay Competition, open to youth 18–25 from all countries of the world, with a top prize of $5,000. These educational organizations and their commercial partners have websites loaded with information and advice.[7]

If you're short on financial information from your family and school, then maybe books, newspaper and magazine articles, TV and other media programs, and Internet sources can fill the gap. The Motley Fool and The Complete Idiot's Guide series of books for teens are especially good. Other popular money books are those by Suze Orman, whose first title, *The 9 Steps to Financial Freedom*, sold 2 million copies. Although Orman's *The Courage to Be Rich* and *The Money Book for the Young, the Fabulous, and the Broke* aren't directed specifically to teenagers, she's done test-marketing research with young people and geared personal appearances to young readers. In her weekly TV show, Orman discusses subjects such as credit scores, credit card management, student loans, home buying, and merging finances with a mate.[8]

Young Money, published every other month by InCharge Institute of America, offers information about personal finance to college-age kids. InCharge also publishes *Military Money* for young adults in military service. The *Wall Street Journal*, probably the best-known daily financial newspaper in the

Newspapers, magazines, and tapes are sources of current information on money matters.

world, publishes a classroom edition nine months a year. This version is often used as a reference by high school teachers, but single subscriptions can be ordered by e-mailing letters.classroom@wsj.com or by calling 1-800-544-0522.

Other print sources of financial information are *Money, Consumer Reports, Kiplinger's Personal Finance Magazine, USA Weekend Magazine,* and occasional articles or columns in *Seventeen, Teen Cosmo, Teen Vogue,* and *O: The Oprah Magazine.*

Oprah Winfrey has also featured money problems on her weekday TV show, such as "Under 21 & In Serious Debt." You can order transcripts and tapes of past shows by going to www.oprah.com/tows/pastshows/tows_past_main.jhtml.

Public television also broadcasts quality programs on money matters. For instance, *Frontline* produced "Merchants of Cool," an hour-long show that examines the methods of marketers who try to exploit teenage culture.[9] Tapes and DVDs of such documentaries are available in some libraries and can be ordered from PBS for $25–$30.

Then there's an entirely different kind of TV money show—MTV's *You Bet I Will*, on which contestants are challenged to perform stunts in exchange for cash. One student was paid to fill his backpack with concrete and carry it around campus all day. Another agreed to drink milk that was strained through a shrimp-and-vinegar-soaked sock.[10] One stunt sponsored by a radio station in January 2007 resulted in the death of Jennifer Strange, 28, who, in an effort to win a Nintendo game for her children, accepted the challenge of drinking so much water that she died of water intoxication. In light of such horror stories, it's not a bad idea to ask yourself on a regular basis what you're willing to do for money and to look for a physically safe, morally comfortable place to draw the line."

No question that you can learn a lot about finances and be entertained at the same time. *Mad about Money*, staged by the National Theatre for Children and Lightbulb Press, amuses and educates middle school students. Without being preachy, in a series of humorous skits, the two-man cast deals with budgeting, borrowing, saving, and investing. Ward Eames, founder of the group, said he wanted to do a play about money because "more young people filed for bankruptcy in 2001 than graduated from college."[12]

If you want to teach yourself about money using only one source, the Internet, you'll find enough material to keep you occupied full-time. Much of it is reliable, useful, and entertaining, but some of it is out-and-out propaganda. Whether you're seeking financial or *any* other kind of information, as we've said repeatedly, you'll need to beware of misinformation and scams. The Internet is amazingly helpful, but "as the greatest boon to information dissemination since the invention of the printing press, it's also the greatest boon to information scams. Because it's so easy to put information on the Internet, it's also easy to find false information," Reid Goldsborough says in "Can the Internet Be Trusted?"[13] A summary of his advice to Internet users follows:

◎ **Think about who is behind the information—a news organization? A money-making organization? A nonprofit organization? An educational institution? An advocacy group?**

TRY THESE INTERNET WEBSITES

Government sites for kids	Sense & Dollars (senseanddollars.thinkport.org)
	LifeSmarts (www.lifesmarts.org)
	The Mint (www.themint.org)
	Young Investor (www.younginvestor.com/kids)
	The AIE Savings Calculator (www.investoreducation.org/cindex2.cfm)
	JumpStart Coalition for Personal Financial Literacy (www.jumpstartcoalition.org)
	The Motley Fool (www.fool.com)
	The Myvesta Foundation (www.myvesta.org)
	InvestorGuide (www.investorguide.com)
For competition	SMG2000: The Stock Market Game (www.smg2000.org) (Invest $100,000 in play money and manage a portfolio of investments)
For girls	Girls Incorporated (www.girlsinc.org)
For fun	Where's George? (www.wheresgeorge.com) (Track and locate a U.S. dollar bill across the country. Enter the serial number and zip code to find out where your dollar bill has been.)

Students? Does the group have an agenda, explicit or hidden? If you aren't familiar with the creators of a website, don't assume they deserve your trust.

◎ Think about whether the information seems reasonable—in keeping with what you already know. If it varies widely from your current understanding, try to verify it with at least two other sources.

◎ Think about the position and appearance of the website. Coming up first on a list doesn't necessarily mean it's the best or even the most popular. A site may be prominent merely because the creators have paid for top billing.

◎ Think about whether the information you're reading is new or old. Check the last update. "A lot of deadwood data is floating around in cyberspace at websites that haven't been updated in several years," Reid Goldsborough says.[14]

◎ Think about substance. Don't judge by the appearance of a website alone. On the other hand, Goldsborough comments, "a site that looks slopped together may include information that's been sloppily researched and presented."[15]

 Be skeptical but not cynical about what you see on the Net. Don't assume that all information is unreliable, but be on your guard.

In conclusion, if you like the idea of rolling in money, take advantage of as many sources with money information as possible.

NOTES

1. Dara Duguay, "Financial Literacy Improves among Nation's High School Students," April 1, 2004, www.financial-education-icfe .org/children_and_money/financial-literacy-improves-among-nations-high-school-students.asp (accessed October 17, 2004).

2. Humphrey Taylor, "When It Comes to Teaching Teens about Managing Money, Mothers Play a Bigger Role Than Fathers," Harris Interactive, Poll #21, April 29, 1998, www.harrisinteractive.com/ harris_poll/index.asp?PID=187 (accessed October 16, 2004).

3. "Survey Shows Teenagers Want Financial Advice from Parents," Consumer@ction, October 23, 2003, www.consumer-action .org/English/PressReleases/2003_10_23_PR.php (accessed September 5, 2004).

4. Robert T. Kiyosaki, *Rich Dad, Poor Dad for Teens* (New York: Warner Books, 2004), 90–91.

5. National Endowment for Financial Education, "Personal Finance Courses in High Schools on the Rise," September 27, 2005, www.nefe.org/news/news092705.html (accessed April 10, 2006).

6. Duguay, "Financial Literacy Improves."

7. Junior Achievement, www.ja.org/about/about_who_vision .shtml (accessed April 19, 2006).

8. "News from Suze," *Publishers Weekly*, December 13, 2004, 28.

9. "The Merchants of Cool," PBS *Frontline*, FROL1909, aired 2004.

10. "Students Exchange Self-Respect for Money on MTV Shows," *Young Money*, www.youngmoney.com/entertainment/ television/020605_01 (accessed April 19, 2006).

11. "Woman Drinks So Much Water She Dies," *CNN.com*, January 13, 2007, www.cnn.com/2007/US/01/13/water.intox.ap/ index.html.

12. Phyllis Furman, "Kids Learn about Money," *New York Daily News*, September 30, 2005, 77.

13. Reid Goldsborough, "Can the Internet Be Trusted?" n.d., www.bcfm.com/financial_manager/Aug%20Sept%2002/Can%20the %20Internet%20Be%20Trusted.htm (accessed April 20, 2006), 1.

14. Goldsborough, "Can the Internet Be Trusted?" 1.

15. Goldsborough, "Can the Internet Be Trusted?" 1.

14 Family and Friends: Avoiding Money Hassles

FAMILY AND MONEY

Where did you get your first nickel, and where did you develop your attitude toward money? From my family, for better or worse, most people would say. Some families get it right. "I haven't experienced any hassles concerning money with my brothers," says McLester, age 18. "We actually help each other." That's the ideal. If your own story involves money tension between you and your parents, or you and your siblings, you're in the majority.

Some disagreements are hostile and long-lasting. "I resent my dad," says an anonymous 17-year-old, "for not giving me money for college. As soon as I asked him he abandoned me as his daughter."

Sometimes factors beyond the family cause tension. "My father and mother both lost jobs at the same time," says Julian, age 18. "You want to go out with friends and eat with them, but you can't. It's tough to tell who should have the money and which reason is better."

Most typically, though, kids and parents argue over temporary and trivial money matters. "I'm actually still on the run from my dad regarding a rather large purchase of CDs on his credit card," says Daniel, age 17. "I try to lay low when he brings it up."

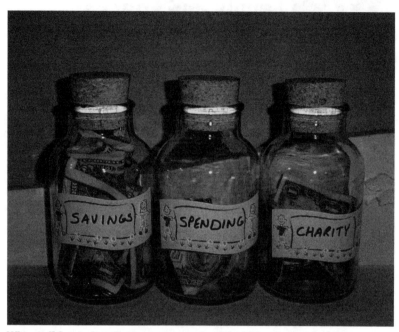

Where did you develop your current attitude toward money?

Money Stirs Up Emotions

You're probably aware by now that money is an emotionally loaded topic. According to psychotherapist Olivia Mellan, money is "never just money, a tool to accomplish one's goals. It is love, power, happiness, security, control, dependency, independence, freedom and more."[1] If money is truly all those things, family members who feel deprived of love, power, security, or independence may overlook actual causes and think that their deprivation has to do with bucks.

Family troubles, even if they aren't caused by money, often result in financial fallout. When families break up, because of divorce or the death of a parent, money problems often appear. Single-parent families are often hard-pressed, and the remarriage of a parent may also complicate finances. Some families are comfortable discussing these matters and others aren't. "My dad and stepmom constantly complain to me about money issues," says Emily, 17, "but my mom and stepdad are more vague on the subject."

"I have a stepfather," Daniel, 17, says, "and it's fine to say that I never ask him for money, not even a ride."

Intimate talk about money is tough for many families. "Information-based money discussions are so taboo," according to Olivia Mellan, "that we usually reach adulthood without a realistic sense of our family's finances."[2] She gives accounts of children affected in negative ways by their parents' anxiety about money—stammering, depression, or addiction to shopping. On the other hand, when families share financial information with their children and speak openly and appropriately about money concerns, kids are likely to learn how to manage money and to feel more secure.

Family Crises

If your parent should have a serious health crisis, lose a job, or face bankruptcy, you will obviously need extra coping skills. That parent may be angry and frustrated and treat you accordingly. Aside from offering extra patience and understanding, you might also offer to get a part-time job, if you don't already have one. An unemployed parent may not

ALMOST ALL FAMILIES HAVE A STORY TO TELL
What can you do if money battles rage in your family?
Listen to all sides and give an opinion if it's wanted. Identify mistakes of others and avoid making the same ones yourself. Offer emotional and practical support if it's appreciated. Keep yourself removed from the battle when possible. You won't do yourself, or anyone, much good if you're among the casualties.

want to accept your financial contribution to the household, but certainly the offer would make that parent feel good. Other gestures that would show your support would be conserving on the use of appliances, eating less expensively, and cutting down on phone calls, entertainment, and clothes.

Sibling Rivalry

Sibling rivalry is usually a fairly mild form of family warfare. "We often fight over money," says Kimberlee, age 18, "because, since I'm older, I get more."

"I'm more spoiled than my older brother," Reisa, age 17, confesses. "He used to joke about it, but I think it was his true feeling."

Sibling rivalry escalates a notch with Kenneth, age 17, who says, "My sister steals money out of my wallet all the time, and we get into heated arguments because she refuses to pay me back."

Is sibling rivalry inevitable or are there ways to get over it? TV's Dr. Phil offers the following comments:[3]

- If you're afraid to trust your sibling and to be open, ask yourself if the problem could be with you. Trust yourself to "come out from behind your wall, deal with what happens, and love them through it."
- If you compete with siblings, you are competing with people on your own team. "Family members should be your support system, not the people with whom you are at odds."
- If you're jealous of a sibling, "ask yourself if you're resentful of his or her success—or whether you just have a need that isn't being met. If you need your sibling to acknowledge, explain, or apologize for something, tell him or her."
- If you have to compete, try to be the "bigger one." Take the high ground and say, "I'm going to love you, whether you like it or not."

Dr. Phil's advice calls for you to be extremely generous, but as he says, "If you lost your sibling today, how significant would your complaints about them be?"

The Problem of "Too Rich"

How about this rare family money problem: a family member wins the lottery and suddenly you're too rich. "When I was growing up," says Sharon Rupinen, age 18, "my family didn't have very much money. . . . All of that changed in January 2000 when my mom won a $21 million Colorado Lotto jackpot. My friends were sort of uneasy because they thought I was going to change. My first boyfriend even broke up with me."[4] Happily Sharon figured out how to keep her friends, she doesn't live extravagantly, and she finds it nice not to have to worry about money anymore.

FRIENDS AND MONEY

You *have* to deal with your family, but friends you can choose, right? Even the best of friends is sometimes annoying, and sometimes money is involved. A typical complication is this: "When going out with a large group of friends," says Melanie, age 17, "there is always some argument over who paid enough, and I usually end up paying more than I should because I deal with the check."

It's hard to organize a large group that may never involve the same people twice. But if, like Melanie, you find yourself repeatedly stuck, try suggesting a system before you enter a restaurant. Ask for separate checks if the waiter can do it. Or pool money ahead of time. Or take turns dealing with the bill. If all fails, avoid eating out with those who don't cooperate.

Borrowing and lending between friends is a potential source of friction. Sometimes givers are willing but receivers are not. Gabriella, age 17, for instance, says, "I have a friend who doesn't have much money, and our friends have no problem buying her pizza or bus fare. But she doesn't want anyone to pay for her."

Avram, age 17, says, "I hang out with kids who have a lot more spending money than I have. This can be very uncomfortable for me."

In other cases, both lenders and borrowers seem contented. "If my friend has less money and wants to borrow a small amount," says Ashley, age 17, "I have no problem lending it. For example, one of my friends wanted a blazer but didn't have enough, so a couple of us chipped in and bought it for her."

Many kids are comfortable lending small amounts to close friends. Ysmael, age 18, says, "I usually just spot a friend the money with faith that they will pay me back. I don't concern myself if they don't. I don't let money get in the way of friendship."

The height of let-it-be attitude is illustrated by Jordan, age 17, who says, "I owe a lot of people money and I don't pay them back. Then again, a lot of people owe me money that I'll never see."

Of course, not everyone can afford to subsidize other people, and some who can afford to lend have objections anyway. "Usually I have more money than my friends," Emily, age 17, reports, "and they often give me the guilt trip about lending to them. One friend was always asking and never paid me back, and when I jokingly mentioned she probably owed me $100 or more, she got angry and defensive, insisting she owed no more than $25."

When Borrowing Creates Problems

Borrowing often results in bad feelings. Kids who sponge all the time get a bad reputation. Those who can't afford to lend are embarrassed, and those with money can be sensitive, too. Bryan, age 17, says, "My friend who has more money than most will consistently deny it when we tell him he's rich. He doesn't want to be labeled as 'the rich kid.'"

Danielle, age 16, adds, "People often assume my family is rich and comment upon it. I never know how to respond."

The more you learn about money dealings the clearer it becomes that borrowing is best when arranged with a bank.

Money and Dating

What about dating someone whose family has a lot more, or a lot less, money than yours has? A *USA Weekend* teen survey shows that "among teens who date, about half say they've dated someone from a family richer than theirs. A third have dated someone from a much poorer family." Eight out of 10 claim that the disparity didn't matter, because "as America grows more multicultural, teenagers are more comfortable dating across all sorts of lines—including economic ones. Money may matter less because teens across the board have more of it, experts say. . . . Mark, 14, agrees. His girlfriend's family is much better off than his, but he concludes, 'It's just not an issue.'"[5]

What will count for more than the net worth of you and another person in a long-term relationship will be whether you two share basically the same values. For instance, will you have similar answers to questions like this?

- What kind of work do we want to do, and will we be satisfied with living on our earnings?
- How do we want to live? What kind of home and material possessions do we feel we can't do without?
- What size family do we want and what expenses will that mean?
- To what extent, and in what way, should we prepare for emergencies and for the future?
- Will we consider what each of us earns as *our* money, or will we keep separate accounts? Will we consult each other on all money decisions?
- How generous do we want to be to family and friends?

If you and your partner-to-be are of the same mind on these matters, you'll probably avoid major financial hassles. Since disagreements about money are often the cause of marital tension and divorce, however, if you and a partner are at opposite ends of the pole, you'll need discussion, expert advice, practical experience, and possibly counseling. Sometimes a spender matched up with a saver results in good compromise, but if partners are fixated on opposing paths, trouble is likely to surface.

Some say that men and women see money differently. Men, according to some psychologists, are more likely to see the world as competitive. They may be less willing than women to share in financial decisions. In a recent survey of high school students, girls saw themselves as less able with math and money, but in fact they knew just as much as the boys.[6] Now that women are gaining social and economic power, surely couples will find it easier to make joint decisions.

GIVING PERSONAL GIFTS

One area for potential problems with both family and friends is in the realm of gift giving. Can you afford to buy gifts? How much should you spend? What if your gift isn't appreciated? What if you receive one you can't stand? What if your sibling gets a better gift than you get? Smart families establish guidelines so that gift giving is fun and not an exercise in resentment. If you feel jealousy, annoyance, embarrassment, or any kind of tension at gift-giving time, it's worth initiating a discussion with your family to express what you feel.

Giving gifts to friends can be equally complicated. Have you ever thought, "I can't give her *that* gift. She'll think I'm cheap!" "I have friends from many different walks of life," says Julia, age 17, "but I feel embarrassed when I'm the one who doesn't give the nicer gift."

Daniel agrees. "I always freeze up when someone who's not a family member gives me a gift. I never know what to give in return, and I become embarrassed, thinking that my gift isn't going to be good enough. So I end up not getting anybody anything."

Clarissa, age 16, doesn't worry about appearances. "I admire cheap people a lot," she says. "It takes a lot of nerve."

Some teens today are in the habit of giving money or gift certificates to friends. Others find that practice to be impersonal or embarrassing. There's great potential for embarrassment on big occasions such as "sweet sixteen" parties when some guests give expensive gifts and less affluent ones spend less. If you can't, or choose not to, give a blockbuster material gift, there's usually a personalized, sentimental choice that will be appreciated as much or more. Possible substitutes are taking the friend to dinner, taking photographs at the party, or ordering from a catalog a personalized item that suits the needs of your friend.

Ideally, family and friends will love you whether or not you have money. Return the favor and value them not for their net worth but for themselves.

NOTES

1. Olivia Mellan and Karina Piskaldo, "Men, Women, and Money," *Psychology Today*, January/February 1999, www.psychologytoday.com/articles/index.php?term=pto-19990101-000035.xml&prin, 1 (accessed May 2, 2006).

2. Mellan and Piskaldo, "Men, Women, and Money," 2.

3. Dr. Phil, "Getting Over Sibling Rivalry," drphil.com/articles/article/329, 1 (accessed June 20, 2006). Direct quotes in the list are all from page 1 of this source.

4. "They're in the Money," *Teen People*, June/July 2003.

5. Patricia Edmonds, "Love & Money," *USA Weekend*, May 2, 1999, www.usaweekend.com/99_issues/990502/990502teenlove.html (accessed March 5, 2005).

6. Mellan and Piskaldo, "Men, Women, and Money," 4.

15 Looking Ahead: Money and Your Future

After living a Stone Age life for centuries, a group of 80 Nukak-Maku people recently wandered out of a forest in Colombia, South America, and declared themselves ready to join the modern world. They had no experience with so-called civilization and no knowledge of money. The only one of the group who had ever been in the outside world and who, as a result spoke some Spanish, seemed baffled by the concept of future. "The future? What's that?" he asked.[1]

> **"Are you doing anything now to prepare for your financial future?"**
>
> **"I have a bank account and some money in CDs, or so my parents tell me. But I never really make any active decisions in the handling of that money. It's like my birthday and graduation checks enter a black hole, never to return."—Daniel, age 17**

Do you know anyone born and raised in America who might say the same thing?

It's hard to plan when the future is uncertain. And aren't philosophers always telling us to make the most of the moment? So if you haven't given much thought yet to higher education, careers, housing, taxes, insurance, and retirement, you have plenty of teenage company. Let's hope, though, that, like the Nukaks, you will take on the modern world and meet its challenges with optimism.

CHOOSING A CAREER

Of course a little planning ahead never hurts. The decision of whether to go for higher education—and where to go and how to pay for it—may be haunting you right now. Libraries are full of books and articles advising you whether or not to go to college or vocational school, how to get accepted, and how to pay. Besides family and teachers who give you advice for nothing, there are services that charge for their help. In a word, there's no shortage of advice for those who want it. We'll stay focused here on the financial aspects of choosing a career.

Some people pick a career path because they think it will bring them a lot of money. Teenagers often claim to want to be doctors, lawyers, or sports figures, jobs they associate with wealth. But since success in those fields requires so much more than just a desire for money, most realistic people end up going after jobs that seem to be suitable, interesting, and available. Loving your work is a great thing. Still, even if you decide to pursue a line of work just because you love it, it's smart to find out in advance what the financial prospects are.

WHAT COLOR IS YOUR COLLAR?

Whether it's fair or not, brainwork is usually rewarded more generously than physical work. White-collar workers— professionals and many office, sales, and government employees—are called by that name because their work is relatively clean and they dress to meet the public. The term *blue-collar*—used to describe carpenters, masons, plumbers, electricians, and so on—refers to the uniforms or work clothes that certain skilled workers wear. A third category designated by the U.S. Department of Labor is "service occupations," which includes guards, waitresses, hair dressers, dental assistants, and porters. In a survey of July 2004, "white-collar workers, who averaged $22.34 per hour, were the highest paid among the three major occupational groups. Blue-collar pay averaged $15.46 per hour, while the pay of service occupations averaged $10.65."[2]

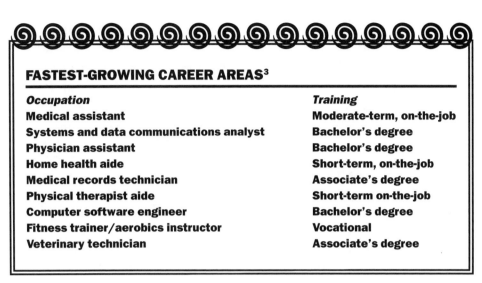

FASTEST-GROWING CAREER AREAS[3]

Occupation	Training
Medical assistant	Moderate-term, on-the-job
Systems and data communications analyst	Bachelor's degree
Physician assistant	Bachelor's degree
Home health aide	Short-term, on-the-job
Medical records technician	Associate's degree
Physical therapist aide	Short-term on-the-job
Computer software engineer	Bachelor's degree
Fitness trainer/aerobics instructor	Vocational
Veterinary technician	Associate's degree

HIGHER EDUCATION AND EARNINGS

It's common knowledge that your lifetime earnings are likely to increase if you pursue education after high school. According to the U.S. Census Bureau, over an adult's working life high school graduates earn an average of $1.2 million; associate's degree holders earn about $1.6 million; and bachelor's degree holders earn about $2.1 million. A master's degree holder would average $2.5 million, and holders of doctoral and professional degrees would average over $4 million. (Note that these figures are based on the value of the dollar in 1999.[4]) The point is that even though the cost of higher education is scary, statistics show that the return is worth the investment.

Of course, the amount you make in your life will be based on several factors, such as what you study, the grades you earn, the exact job you get, how hard you work, how original you are, where your job is located, and the state of the economy. But no matter how many years you've spent in school or how good your other credentials are, earning a top salary isn't guaranteed.

OTHER BENEFITS OF HIGHER ED

College experience pays off in a lot of ways that aren't strictly monetary. Research shows that people who have attended college have greater personal and professional mobility, better quality of life for their kids, and more hobbies and leisure activities. College attendance has been shown to "decrease prejudice, enhance knowledge of world affairs, and enhance social status," and "college graduates appear to have a more optimistic view of their past and future personal progress."[5]

VOCATIONAL EDUCATION

College, naturally, isn't the only post–high school choice. Vocational education is a solid alternative. "Vocational education in general . . . is trying to move on from its past. . . . It is not even called vocational education anymore; now the official term is career and technical education, or CTE for short. The curriculum focuses on newer careers, such as computers and 'informational technology.' Students must get hands-on experience and pass certification exams devised at least partly by the industries that employ them."[6] If you type "trade schools" into an Internet search engine, you'll find directories that list nearly 250 different training programs in schools all over the country, programs that include accounting, baking and pastry, funeral service, personal trainer, real estate broker, collision repair, skin care, wedding consultant, and dozens more.

AND IF YOU *DON'T* PURSUE HIGHER ED?

Dropouts from high school, college, and vocational school sometimes beat the odds. A *Forbes* magazine article, for instance, states that "58 members of the Forbes 400 [very high earners] either avoided college or dropped out partway through their schooling." These members, including Bill Gates, are reported to have more than twice the net worth of Forbes 400 members who went to Ivy League colleges.[7]

COMPARATIVE EARNINGS OF MEN AND WOMEN

Although many individual women these days earn as much as, or more than, men in the same jobs, females in general still

Table 15.1. Incomes of Men and Women in 2003[8]

Occupation	Average Income for Women	Average Income for Men
Lawyer	$73,000	$84,000
Pharmacist	71,000	80,000
Marketing and sales manager	47,000	66,000
Maid or cleaner	16,000	19,000
Waitress or waiter	17,000	20,000
Teacher assistant	18,000	22,000

make less money than men. Women in the past stayed at home, but their gradual entrance into the workforce intensified during World War II (1941–1945) and continues today. Some incomes of women compared to those of men working in the same field can be found in table 15.1.

In short, it's an exception for a woman to earn more than most men in her field. Still, the gap between the genders is narrowing. The proportion of women in managerial jobs has increased as well.[9] According to a 2006 Junior Achievement Poll, girls aiming at careers in medicine, business, and education expect higher earnings than boys expect.[10] Will those high expectations help them achieve equality some day soon?

MOST POPULAR CAREERS

Which career goals are most appealing these days? When Gallup pollsters in 2005 asked more than 1,000 kids age 13–17 to pick favorite careers, the most popular fields were teaching, medicine, law, sports, science, architecture, business, military, engineering, and nursing. As you can imagine, choices varied by gender. Girls put teaching at the top and boys, sports. The military was more popular with males and nursing ranked higher with females. Preferences change over time. In a poll taken about 30 years ago, the top job choice for boys was skilled worker (carpenter, plumber, electrician) and the girls' top choice was secretary.[11]

HOW MUCH CAN YOU MAKE?[12]

Since salaries vary from place to place and year to year, the following examples are useful mostly in terms of ranking. That is, the average income of a dentist, which appears close to the top of this list, will remain higher than the income of a dental hygienist, regardless of place and time. Because they are averages, from all over the United States, with a percentage of error built in, and with extras such as tips excluded, some actual incomes were considerably higher than shown here.

Occupation	Average Earnings in 2004
Physician	$129,000
Airplane pilot	128,000
Judge	121,000
Lawyer	106,000
Dentist	82,000
Engineer	76,000
Architect	68,000
Real estate salesperson	65,000
Computer programmer	60,000
Physical therapist	58,000
Dental hygienist	56,000
Buyer, wholesale or retail	55,000
Registered nurse	53,000
Detective	50,000
Plumber	47,000
Firefighter	47,000
Teacher	47,000
Carpenter	40,000
Auto mechanic	39,000
Construction worker	35,000
Practical nurse	34,000
Welder	34,000
Sanitation worker	31,000
Bookkeeper	30,000
Gardener, nursery worker	24,000
Counter clerk	21,000
Cab driver	20,000
Food preparer	16,000
Waiter/waitress	9,000

FINDING OUT ABOUT CAREERS

Regardless of what occupation you're considering, it pays to check out, online or in print, the U.S. Department of Labor's *Occupational Outlook Handbook (OOH)*. The *OOH* provides information on necessary training and education, earnings, expected job prospects, what workers do on the job, working conditions, and job search tips. This nationally recognized source is revised every two years.[13] *Apprenticeship* by Penny Hutchins Paquette in the same series as this book is another source to explore.

CAREERS IN THE MILITARY

The biggest employer of all in the United States is the military. No other branch of government, nor any corporation, has as many employees as Uncle Sam does—about a million and a half. Traditionally many men and increasing numbers of women have joined the service as a route to financial security and educational opportunities. Other benefits of a military career are equality of opportunity; free housing, food, clothing, and medical care; on-the-job training; 30-days leave per year; regular salary increases; travel; tuition assistance; and good pensions and early retirement. In peacetime these benefits are attractive. Negatives of a military career—in addition to the obvious risk of physical harm—are the need to live a regimented life and to go where you're sent.

How much can you earn in the military? About the same amount or a little more than you'd make for comparable jobs in the private sector. Which branch pays the best? "The basic pay is the same for every branch of service. Checks are issued twice a month. The amount follows a table issued by the Department of Defense that breaks down the numbers according to ranking scale and length of service. . . . For a look at it, check out militarypay.dtic.mil. As an example, in the spring of 2002 the E-3 rank for Private First Class (low pay) was about $1,214 a month, and high pay (O-8 rank—commissioned officer) was about $6,838 a month, for less than two years of service.[14]

COLLEGE OR NOT?

So, should you spend big bucks for higher education or not? In terms of getting a good-paying job, the 2020 Commission of the Future of Post-Secondary Education concludes that in our century, "higher education will become increasingly important for landing high-paying jobs. But for the foreseeable future, many jobs will require no formal schooling beyond high school."[15]

UNEMPLOYMENT

Let's hope you find work that you like and stay employed as long as you want to. Unfortunately though, even if you're well trained, hardworking, and determined, at some point you may experience bad luck. The economy runs in cycles. If you were between the ages of 20 and 24 in the year 2000, for instance, you would have found 6.7 percent of your age group unemployed. But three years later, in 2003, 10.9 percent of that age group were unemployed.[16] Nationally, unemployment rates for all ages depend on exact time and place, with the national rate of November 2006 at 4.5 percent.[17]

A silver lining is that, if you've worked at a job long enough and you lose it through no fault of your own, you're entitled to apply for unemployment compensation, or a modest weekly income. This program is overseen by the federal government but run by each state, so eligibility, how much you receive, and how much tax you pay will vary. To be eligible in the first place, you have to be working for an employer who pays into the program. The compensation you receive will be a percentage of your former earnings and will be paid for only a limited amount of time.

NO PLACE LIKE HOME

Okay, the future has arrived. You have a job. You have your own place to live—or do you? As a newcomer to the job market, maybe you'll find yourself in the position of Anna, age 25, a college student with a part-time job, who moved back in with her parents in Kensington, Maryland. "'She was having trouble making ends meet,' says her mother Patricia. 'It's hard to pay for health insurance, student loans, and rent on part-time pay.'"[18]

"Census figures show that 56 percent of men and 43 percent of women ages 18 to 24 today live with one or both parents. Some never left, while an estimated 65 percent of recent college graduates have moved back in with their parents."[19] A portion of these so-called boomerang kids go home briefly to get their finances in order. Others get so comfortable that they lose the motivation to become independent.

GETTING YOUR OWN PLACE

The right time for getting your own place will depend on a lot of factors, such as your relationship with your family, the security of your income, the cost of living in your area, and whether or not you're sharing expenses. The thought of spending your own money for all necessities and extras may slow you down in looking for a place of your own. Renters in 2001 spent 29 percent of their income on their homes.[20]

Chances are that your first experience living away from your family will be in rental housing. Sharing an apartment or house with one or more friends obviously saves money, and if you don't know anyone to share with, you can advertise. Colleges, places of worship, or social organizations sometimes post home-sharing notices. These days, roommate searches are often conducted on the Internet, and popular sites that claim to screen applicants are www.EasyRoommate.com, www.roommates.com, and www.roommateclick.com. Often the person who already has an apartment places an ad to be answered by interested parties who describe themselves via e-mail. (For instance, "single female nonsmoker who goes to bed early.")

Kathy, several years out of college, says,

> I've had a very positive experience with a roommate I met on the Internet through Craigslist, which brings people together with similar interests and lifestyles. We have a great deal in common. I suspect that part of this is serendipity. I can't imagine that most roommates "bond" by listening to North Korean pop music and

boston rooms & shares classifieds and want ads - craigslist

Page 1 of 5

boston craigslist > rooms & shares
boston | boston/camb/brook | north west | metro west | north shore | south/southeast   [help] [post]

search for: _____   in: [rooms & shares ▾]   Search   ☐ only search titles

rent: [min]   [max]   ☐ cats ☐ dogs

[Sat, 23 Sep 12:16:14]   [housing forum] [**cashier check & wire transfer scams**]
[stating a discriminatory preference in a housing post is illegal]
[success story?] [**spoofed email warning**] [download firefox]
[full text mode] [defend net neutrality!]

Sat Sep 23

$600 Share Townhouse/Own Bd & Bath (Bradford)

$600 Furnished Room in Townhouse Condo (South Shore) pic

$490 SPACIOUS 1br in a 2br DUPLEX APT IN MEDFORD SQUARE / GREAT AMENITIES! (Medford) pic

$950 ROOM avail. Oct. 1 - HUGE MULTI-LEVEL FURNISHED LUXURY APARTMENT (Somerville) pic

$700 1 BR available in January in 2 BR/1BA Apartment in Davis Sq. Area (Davis Square/Somerville) pic

$550 Stoneham Room Available all Utilities

0 Large Sunny Rooms in Attractive Nice Home img

... 2/2 condo FURNISHED (200 cove way)

Craigslist on the Internet is a useful tool for finding roommates.

decorating their apartment with oversize plastic insects. On the other hand, I've known people who met through Craigslist and hated each other. Thus the need for communication before you actually move in together and honesty from both parties about the living environment they want.

BUYING A HOUSE

Let's leap farther into the future. You've been saving, on your own or with someone else, to buy an apartment or house. What's involved—and why buy instead of rent? Buying means making a down payment—a substantial amount, sometimes as much as 20 percent of the selling price—and taking out a mortgage.

A mortgage is a big loan, to be paid off every month, over years. A small part of the monthly charge goes to pay off the principal (the amount you borrowed), but the larger part is interest—your payment for the privilege of borrowing. The obvious benefit of buying a house is that after a certain number of years, you own it. Your mortgage payments end, and you can

Lara's house in Raleigh, North Carolina

live less expensively or perhaps sell your house at a profit in order to buy a better one.

For example, Lara, age 24, who works for a finance and mortgage company, says,

> I was sharing a rental in Maryland, but when I moved down to Raleigh, North Carolina, and the housing market was more reasonable, it made sense for me to buy instead of rent. Though I'm paying slightly more for a mortgage payment than for my old rent, I'm also building equity. With the local Realtor I searched for houses priced below what I was pre-qualified for, since this is my first time living alone, and I didn't want to feel overextended. I settled on a house that is close to my office, requires little maintenance, and will be easy to sell when I move.

Building equity, as Lara mentions, is a big advantage of home buying. Assuming her house increases in value, as houses usually do, when she sells it, it will be worth more than she paid out. In addition to buying a house for their own use, some people buy houses as investments in the hope that they'll increase in value and can be sold at a profit.

Another benefit of owning a home is that property taxes and interest on a mortgage are tax deductible, which means you may end up paying less income tax than you would as a renter. Consider this point, though: sometimes the economy is in a temporary phase where renting is less expensive than owning an apartment or a house.

Finding the money for a down payment is often a problem. Often, if they can, parents or other relatives help out. Sometimes first-time home buyers or veterans are able to get loans at very low interest rates and can buy a home with less money down. Once you've decided to buy, the next question is buy *what*? A condominium apartment? A cooperative apartment? A town house or a single-family house?

When you're actually ready to buy you'll focus on details. For now, let's just get a general idea of what the terms mean. A condominium apartment may be located in a low-rise or high-rise building. You own your own space in the building and you co-own common areas (halls, roof, swimming pools) with other owners in your building or complex.

Meanwhile, cooperative (or co-op) owners are considered stockholders in a corporation in which they own a certain number of shares. In order to be allowed to buy into the building you'll need the approval of the co-op board of directors. This approval involves proving, through your pay stubs, income tax records, and personal references, that you are a good risk. Co-ops often have stricter regulations than condos concerning what is permitted. For instance, you may find rules in a co-op that prevent you from renting out (sub-letting) your space to someone else. Both condo and co-op owners are assessed a monthly maintenance fee to keep common areas in good shape.

Town house ordinarily describes a single- or multi-story unit that's linked to other units horizontally. As with condos, common areas are owned jointly and are usually managed by a property owners' association.

The American Dream supposedly includes a single-family house with a white picket fence. With or without the fence, 68.9 percent of Americans owned their homes (including apartments) in 2005. The highest rate of homeownership was in the Midwest, and the state with the highest number of homeowners was West Virginia. Lowest rates of homeownership were found in the most expensive areas—the District of Columbia and the states of New York and California.[21]

REAL ESTATE AGENTS

Regardless of whether you're renting or buying an apartment, a town house, or a single-family house, there's a lot to consider. Possibly you'll go to an agent, who will help you find what you're looking for. Agents also assist sellers by finding customers. Agents and their agencies receive a percentage of the sale price as compensation. The percentage varies (usually about 6 percent) and is ordinarily paid by the seller. If an agent arranges a rental, the renter ordinarily pays the fee. The amount varies from state to state but is often 10 percent of the total or about one month's rent.

It's possible to rent, buy, and sell real estate without using an agent. The advantage, of course, is saving the fee. Acting on your own behalf, however, means doing for yourself everything an agent usually does, such as: locating properties and narrowing down possibilities; accumulating reliable information about the property and neighborhood; negotiating (that is, bargaining—making an offer and coming to an agreement about the price); and finding inspectors, lawyers, and bank personnel to conclude the sale (the closing).

Some questions to think about when buying a home are, How much can I afford—including up-front and ongoing expenses? What size and style do I want? Is property size important to me? Is the location convenient to work, transportation, stores, and schools? Is the neighborhood appealing and will the house probably gain value? Am I thinking in terms of a lifetime, or is this house a step along the way?

In figuring out how much you can afford to spend for a home, don't forget these expenses:

◎ **Up-front: cost of house itself, inspection, closing costs to lawyers and title companies, renovations, moving, and furnishings**

◎ **Ongoing: monthly mortgage payment, monthly operating costs, property taxes, home insurance, and repairs**

As expensive as homeownership is, Americans believe in it, and the federal government, by way of the U.S. Department of Housing and Urban Development (HUD), is committed to helping low- and moderate-income Americans buy homes. The Federal Housing Administration offers low-interest loans, and HUD provides a Home-Buying Guide and a lot of other information—by mail (451 7th St. S.W., Washington, DC 20410) or on the Internet at FHA.gov and FirstGov.gov.

INSURANCE

Certain adult matters aren't too terrible to think about. Buying houses? Hey, that can be fun. Retirement? Not bad. Look at all the free time you'll have. But health insurance and life insurance are probably not topics that fascinate you at this point. And let's face it, many adults avoid those subjects as well. Take a deep breath now and read a few words that may do you some good later on. Insurance, in general, is protection against financial loss offered by a company that charges you money each year (a premium), and in exchange they agree to compensate you for losses and/or expenses. In addition to health insurance, it's smart to insure your life and your property. There, was that so bad?

If you're lucky, health insurance for you and your family, if and when you have one, will be paid by your employer. These days, unfortunately, many companies require employees to contribute—if they provide medical insurance at all. Health insurance that you have to pay for privately costs thousands of dollars a year, so having it provided by your employers is as good as getting a higher salary.

Millions of people in the United States have no medical coverage, which is bad news for all of us, because, if the uninsured end up in emergency rooms, those who pay taxes will end up paying the high cost. Many citizens and some politicians are working to extend health insurance to all Americans, but so far, high costs and disputes over how to run programs have stood in the way.

LIFE INSURANCE

Almost everybody understands the benefits of health insurance, but being urged to pay for *life* insurance while you're young may be harder to understand. When you buy life insurance you pay a certain amount of money—the premium—periodically, and in return the insurance company agrees to pay a specified amount to your beneficiary when you die. So who needs life insurance most and how does it work?

The main reason to insure your life is if you have a spouse, children, or aging parents who depend on your income. The amount the insurance company pays them at your death will help replace what you would have earned. The younger you are when you take out a policy, the lower the premiums will be that you pay each month or quarter. The exact cost is based on projections of average life expectancy, which, in the United States in 2003, for men and women taken together, was 77.6 years.

You may be able to participate in group life insurance at your job, but lots of people take out a private policy as well. The two basic types of private life insurance are *term* and *whole life*. Term insurance, sometimes called temporary life insurance, gives you protection against loss of life for a certain amount of time. Let's say you need insurance coverage most while your children are young, so you take out a policy for 20 years. Unless you renew at the end of 20 years—and pay a much higher premium because you're older—the policy will end at that time. You will have "lost" the money you paid, but you will have survived!

Whole life insurance, on the other hand, is a permanent policy. You pay a set amount each year as long as you live, or for a specified number of years, and the insurance company will pay the beneficiary a stated sum when you die. In other words, a whole life policy, which usually costs more than term, doesn't run out. It's a form of savings as well as offering a death benefit.

PROPERTY INSURANCE

That home you've bought that cost a fortune? Well, let's say there's an electrical fire. Or pipes burst. Or a tree falls on your garage. If you've been paying all along for a homeowner's insurance policy, you'll be paid for a large part of your losses from such disasters. Most policies also cover you for theft of possessions, although valuable jewelry, antiques, and such usually have to be insured separately. In addition, with most policies, if a house guest slips and is injured or your child breaks something valuable belonging to your neighbor, the personal liability portion of the policy will pay the bills, including legal defense.[22]

MOTOR VEHICLE INSURANCE

As we said in chapter 11, "Ring Tones and Dream Machines," if you own a car you'll need motor vehicle insurance. Most states require you to carry insurance to pay for damage and injury that you cause to people and property. Collision insurance, which costs extra, reimburses you for damage to your own car in an accident. Buying car insurance with good coverage is very expensive. The average yearly cost nationwide of insuring a passenger car in 2003 was over $800.[23] If you own an expensive car and live in a big city, add as much as several thousand dollars to that.

One last thing to keep in mind about homeowners or car insurance is that whenever you make a claim, no matter how justifiable, there's the possibility the premiums of your next policy will go up. And worst-case scenario, if you make too many claims you'll have trouble finding a company willing to insure you at all.

YOU CAN'T AVOID TAXES

Another pain of adulthood is taxes. In life and in this book you can't escape them. I've already mentioned various taxes along the way, but in case you're forgetting, they're collected by a

governmental authority to pay for buildings, personnel,
programs, services, and events that will supposedly benefit us
all. Tax rates vary depending on which politicians are in power.
Sometimes wealthy people are favored and at other times the
little guy gets a break. Even now you're most likely paying sales
taxes on purchases at the mall or in a restaurant (currently,
there are five states with no sales tax: Alaska, Delaware,
Montana, New Hampshire, and Oregon). And if you have a
job, you're paying federal, and perhaps state, income tax, and
you're seeing deductions for Social Security (FICA).

At the moment you probably aren't paying property (real
estate) taxes, but if you own a home someday you'll have to pay
up. The amount, collected by your town, is based on the worth
of your house and grounds, and ordinarily most of the money
goes to pay for local schools. At the point when you own a
home and have kids in public schools, think of your property
taxes as the price of their education.

It's bad enough to be taxed while you're alive and kicking,
right? An estate tax, on the other hand, is "a federal tax
collected on the value of a person's property at the time of his or
her death." Your estate—or what you leave to your survivors—
is made up of your investments, property, and bank accounts.
Whoever inherits your estate may have to pay a tax to the
federal government and to the state. The amount they pay is
based on the total value of what you left behind, minus an
exemption. The exemption varies, but in 2009, for example,
inheritors won't have to pay the federal government on the first
$3.5 million of the estate. In case you're starting to add up the
benefits of marriage, one is that "with careful estate planning,
you may leave all of your property to your surviving spouse,
free of federal estate taxes."[24]

One more tax—on gifts from the living. In case you were
hoping for a relative to give you $100,000 this year—the chances
aren't good. Both federal and state governments impose a tax on
any money gift over $11,000, a tax the donor has to pay. That is,
your grandmother and grandfather together can give you
$22,000 a year without having to pay taxes on it, but if they
insist on giving you more than that, they'll have to pay tax.

Americans complain a lot about taxes. A large percentage of taxpayers think the federal tax system should be changed or completely overhauled. They believe federal taxes are too high and too complicated—even though millions of people who earn little end up paying no taxes, and the taxes of the richest Americans are less now than they were years ago. Critics of the system claim that some of the richest Americans pay the least tax, proportionately. A Harris Interactive poll showed that "59 percent of Americans believe they pay more federal income tax as a percentage of income than billionaire Donald Trump."[25]

RETIREMENT INCOME

If it's hard at this point to picture working for years and paying taxes, it's all that much harder to imagine retirement. With luck, you'll work at a job that eventually provides you with a pension—that is, a source of retirement income paid at least partially by your employer. And assuming you're one of the 97 percent of workers who pays into the FICA system (Social Security), and assuming the system continues as it is now, you'll receive a monthly payment from the federal government, starting when you're between 62 and 70. The longer you wait to collect, the greater the amount of your benefit will be. This system, established in 1935, "is a package of protection that provides benefits to retirees, survivors, and disabled persons. . . . The amount of retirement benefits you receive from Social Security is based on your earnings over the years. The more you work and the higher your earnings, the greater your benefits, up to a certain maximum amount. . . . To qualify for retirement benefits you must earn a certain number of credits."[26] But if you have worked "off the books," without contributing to FICA, you won't be entitled to collect Social Security.

The idea of collecting both a pension and Social Security beginning in your sixties may sound pretty good, but many people, in addition, save on their own for retirement. Retirement comes sooner than anybody thinks it will. Saving even a little bit along the way adds up. Because of medical breakthroughs you may live a long time in retirement, with expenses that may increase. If you've lived comfortably in your working years, you can't rely solely on Social Security or a company pension plan to cover your basic retirement needs. Throughout your retirement, you'll get slight increases in pension and Social Security benefits, but those increases may not be enough to keep up with inflation.

You're likely to hear big debates these days about the Social Security system. Some Americans think that the system may falter or go broke. (When the big population of Baby Boomers retires, some say, there won't be enough younger workers paying into the fund.)

Certain people think the solution is in privatizing Social Security, which means shifting the common pool of funds to individual accounts. Others say that the crisis of Social Security is being exaggerated and can be fixed without upsetting changes. You'll be smart if you follow this debate and express your opinion to your congressional representatives, since the way the debate is resolved will definitely affect your life.

BACK TO THE PRESENT

The financial responsibilities of adulthood may be around the corner, but you have time to prepare and they don't have to weigh you down. If you're sports minded, think of getting money as one of the great games in life. If you love money, make that a good thing and try not to let it rule you. If you see money as the root of problems, do what you can to solve money problems while you're young. If thinking about money bores you, find (hire, if you have to) reliable people to give you advice. If you think of yourself as unlucky with money, strive to change your luck. And if you manage to accumulate more money than you need, find satisfaction in giving to people and causes that you like. Good luck!

NOTES

1. Juan Forero, "Leaving the Wild, and Rather Liking the Change," *New York Times*, May 11, 2006, A1.

2. U.S. Department of Labor, "National Compensation Survey: Occupational Wages in the United States, July 2004," Summary 05-02, August 2005.

3. For the years 2002–2012. Warren Farrell, *Why Men Earn More* (New York: AMACOM, 2005), 119.

4. U.S. Census Bureau, "The Big Payoff: Educational Attainment and Synthetic Estimates of Work-Life Earnings," Special Studies, July 2002, www.census.gov/prod/2002pubs/p23-210.pdf (accessed January 2, 2007).

5. Kathleen Porter, "The Value of a College Degree," *ERIC Digest*, 2002, www.ericdigests.org/2003-3/value.htm, 2–3 (accessed December 19, 2006).

6. Gail Robinson, "Vocational Education," *Gotham Gazette*, February 14, 2005, www.gothamgazette.com/article//20050214/200/1320, 2 (accessed May 31, 2006).

7. Bettina Lankard Brown, "Vocational Certificates and College Degrees," *Eric Digest*, no. 212, 1999, www.ericdigests.org/2000-2/degrees.htm, 2 (accessed May 14, 2006).

8. Farrell, *Why Men Earn More*, 8–11.

9. Bureau of Labor Statistics, "Women at Work: A Visual Essay," Monthly Labor Review, October 2003.

10. "For First Time, Girls' Salary Expectations Are on Par with Boys', According to New Junior Achievement Poll," January 24, 2006, www.jobshadow.org/press/release/pr_012406.html (accessed January 2, 2007).

11. CNNMoney, "Teen Dreams: Top 10 Career Choices," May 26, 2005, www.money.cnn.com/2005/05/17/pf/teen_careers/?cnn=yes (accessed July 16, 2005).

12. John E. Buckley, "Rankings of Full-Time Occupations by Annual Earnings, July 2004," U.S. Department of Labor, Bureau of Labor Statistics, July 2004, www.bls.gov/opub/cwc/cm20051121ar01p1.htm (May 18, 2006).

13. U.S. Department of Labor, *Occupational Outlook Handbook*, www.bls.gov/oco/home.htm (May 18, 2006).

14. Bill Harris, *The Complete Idiot's Guide to Careers in the U.S. Military* (New York: Alpha Books, 2002), 7.

15. Washington Research Council, "The Economic Value of Higher Education," Special Report, July 22, 1999, www.researchcouncil.org/Reports/1999/EconomicValueofHigherEducation/EconomicValueofHigherEducation.htm, 7 (accessed May 13, 2006).

16. New York Life, "Adult Children Moving Back Home," www.newyorklife.com/cda/0,3254,13762,00.html (accessed May 22, 2006).

17. U.S. Department of Labor, www.bls.gov/home.htm (accessed December 19, 2006).

18. Linda Greider, "Hard Times Drive Adult Kids 'Home,'" *AARP Bulletin*, December 2001, www.aarp.org/bulletin/yourlife/a2003-06-26-hardtimes.html?print=yes, 1 (accessed May 22, 2006).

19. New York Life, "Adult Children Moving Back Home," 1.

20. U.S. Census Bureau, "American Housing Survey," www.census.gov/hhes/www/housing/ahs/ahsfaq.html (accessed June 4, 2006).

21. Danter Company, "Home Ownership Rates," www.danter.com/STATISTICS/homeown.htm (accessed June 4, 2006).

22. Jack R. Kapoor, Les R. Dlabay, Robert J. Hughes, and William B. Hoyt, *Business and Personal Finance* (Woodland Hill, CA: Glencoe/McGraw Hill, 2005), 465–69, 420–22.

23. Insurance Information Institute, www.iii.org/media/facts/statsbyissue/auto/ (accessed June 5, 2006).

24. Kapoor et al., *Business and Personal Finance*, 512.

25. Robert Longley, "Most Americans Feel They Pay More Taxes Than Trump," usgovinfo.about.com/od/incometaxandtheirs/a/taxtrump.htm, 1 (accessed June 6, 2006).

26. Kapoor et al., *Business and Personal Finance*, 486.

Appendix:
Answers to Quizzes

ANSWERS FOR PAGE VII

1. D. All were used, but the most popular were Spanish silver dollars, or pieces of eight, which could be cut into eight bits. Some people today still call a quarter "two bits."
2. B. The government printed continentals during the American Revolution. They printed so many that they weren't worth much.
3. B. The same law created a first national mint (where coins are made) in Philadelphia.
4. D. Meanwhile, Washington is on the $1 bill, Lincoln the $5, and Jackson the $20.
5. B. Most worn-out bills are replaced with new ones. The government used to burn damaged bills, but they stopped to cut air pollution.

ANSWERS FOR PAGE 76

1. A
2. B
3. D
4. D
5. B
6. C

ANSWERS FOR PAGE 106

The front pair is $3, the middle pair is $17, and the back pair is $117.

Index

Index

About the Author

Robin F. Brancato was born in Reading, Pennsylvania; graduated from the University of Pennsylvania; and has spent her adult life writing and teaching. She is the mother of two sons and the author of eight young adult books, including *Uneasy Money*. She currently lives with her husband, John, in Fort Lee, New Jersey.